MODESTLY

10 9 8 7 6 5 4 3 2

Ebury Press, an imprint of Ebury Publishing,
20 Vauxhall Bridge Road,
London, SW1V 2SA

Ebury Press is part of the Penguin Random House group of companies
whose addresses can be found at global.penguinrandomhouse.com

Penguin
Random House
UK

First published by Ebury Press in 2018

www.penguin.co.uk

A CIP catalogue record for this book is available from the British Library

Publishing Director: Lizzy Gray
Project Editor: Louise McKeever
Designer: Imagist
Production: Helen Everson and Rebecca Jones
Photography: Claire Pepper © pages 4, 6, 65, 67, 71, 73, 74, 75, 76, 77, 78, 79,
84, 85, 86, 87, 88, 89, 93, 95, 98, 101, 107, 131, 132, 134, 135, 140, 143, 152, 156, 160,
161, 162, 163, 164, 187, 192, 220
Alessia Gammarota © pages 8, 25, 26, 27, 29, 41, 53, 56, 59, 61, 69, 82, 102, 122,
126, 127, 128, 129, 198, 209

ISBN: 978-1-785-03527-2

Colour origination by Rhapsody Ltd London
Printed and bound in Italy by L.E.G.O. S.p.A.

Penguin Random House is committed to a sustainable future for
our business, our readers and our planet. This book is made from
Forest Stewardship Council® certified paper.

DINA TORKIA

MODESTLY

EBURY
PRESS

CONTENTS

006 **Introduction**

008 **My Journey**

066 **Fashion**

140 **Beauty**

166 **Parenting & Family**

186 **Dina's Reflections**

220 **Dina's Final Thoughts**

222 **Index**

Introduction

This is a story about life. Well, my life so far. It's about a series of unpredictable turns. It's about me as a Muslim Brit embracing dual identities, surviving the turbulent teens and transitioning from self-doubt to self-belief.

There is a little bit of drama, we may even shed a few tears together, but more importantly there will be a lot of laughs (mainly me laughing at myself). And, of course, the inescapable shedload of bold statements. You can't get a Muslim woman in a hijab with no opinion, am I right?! Even if they are mainly fashion ones…

This journey of mine, well, it's still a wide-open road, and I want to take you with me. Some of you have already been walking with me – even running like mad at times – but now I want to take a moment to look back on all the craziness and take a deep breath.

Right, let's go.

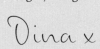

My Journey

THE OTHER HALF

'In order to be irreplaceable, one must always be different.'

Coco Chanel

Let me introduce you to the term 'halfie'. Halfie is a term used by me, my twin sister and my group of friends for someone who is half this and half that – like me. I'm half Egyptian, half English.

I was born in Egypt, Cairo, in 1989 to an Egyptian dad and an English mama. Some of my earliest childhood memories are filled with pyramids, dust and donkeys. Yep, I'm feeding the stereotype there. While much of the city is indeed dust, it's also crammed to the brim with the busiest streets and wildest traffic jams you'll ever see. In short, Cairo is a load of fun, sun and a whole lotta character.

England was also very much part of my upbringing. We spent many holidays with my maternal grandparents and extended family, until eventually holidays became something more permanent – my parents decided to move to England. I was six years old at the time.

Unlike most kids, I wasn't actually too worried about moving abroad and having to fit in. Having a mother who is English and having spent my childhood in Egypt meant my twin and I grew up in an environment infused with both Egyptian and British culture. And language wasn't a problem either, as we were fluent in Arabic and English. So moving to Britain never felt daunting, it felt exciting.

Although we would miss our Egyptian relatives dearly – especially our cousins, who were the same age as us, we were also looking forward to starting a new school, a new life and spending more time with our maternal grandparents.

We joined in Year 2 at our new primary school in London. The school run was a big contrast to the long, exhaustingly hot car journeys that we were so used to. In London we got there in seconds, as we were literally neighbours with the school gates.

On my first day I waltzed through those gates in a bright orange, floral-printed summer dress – a far cry from the baby blue pinstripe dresses all the other girls were wearing. My mum had yet to pick up our school uniforms, but it was fine! I chose what to wear myself that day and I had my sister by my side, so I really wasn't too worried.

Then the inevitable happened – for the first time ever I was put in a separate class to my twin. I walked into the classroom alone, not knowing what to expect. But then I breathed a sigh of relief – and surprise – to see the diversity of my classmates. It's safe to say I fitted in there more than I ever did amongst the kids in our Cairo class, which was only filled with Egyptian kids. Yeah, I was half Egyptian, but because I was also half English, I spoke English differently to them, and so I never completely blended in. In the London school, there were lots of people like us: Indians, Arabs, white kids, black kids, eastern European, mixed-race kids, so we felt it was a much more natural fit.

I quickly made a best friend, as you do at that age. Her name was Nisha Chavda and we did everything together, both in school and out. With a new best friend by my side, a mix of kids from different backgrounds – and not forgetting a quick school run – primary school days flew past in a carefree roller coaster ride of friends, excitement and learning.

Amid all that, my two younger brothers also came on the scene during my primary years. The older one was born when I was six, and the younger when I was eight. So being a responsible older sister was also in full swing!

The four of us have always been close, even if we are different. My brothers are not alike at all, just like my sister and I – we are like chalk and cheese! But we love hanging out together, and I think that our differences in character have meant that both my brothers and my sister have always been my friends as well as my siblings.

We were always a team, and I still remember how the four of us used to attend Arabic school together on a Saturday. I absolutely hated it; the teachers were too strict and the syllabus was so difficult to follow. My sister, brothers and I used to get up to no good, making fun of the teachers and generally misbehaving. We used to bunk off lessons as much as possible along with our fellow halfie Egyptian mates.

My siblings and I appreciate the fact that being a halfie means having memorable experiences on both sides of our cultures. Holidays were spent either in Egypt or on a weekend away in Wallasey, Merseyside, with our grandparents. Some of my fondest memories are from the Mersey coast – the long brisk walks with the dog along the seashore, the fish and chips on the pier and being knee-deep in water scouring for crabs.

On the other side, in Egypt, holidays were very different but just as fun. When we were in Cairo for Eid, we'd get a goody bag of treats from our Egyptian grandma, whom we called 'teta'. Then we'd go up to the balcony with our cousins to throw down firecracker balls. After our antics, we'd watch the non-stop street parties go by: the parade of horses dressed in bright colours, the bustling crowds of happy families and the standstill traffic that played a cacophony of tooting car horns!

Back in London, Eid wasn't quite as crazy, but it had its own flavour – the community would

get together and eat endless plates of food, there'd be Eid parties at Regent's Park mosque and lots of *eidiyya* – money that elders give to the youngsters – which I (of course) loved!

Eid wasn't the only highlight of my childhood. Again, my dual upbringing meant I was able to enjoy non-Muslim traditions, too, and Christmas was big in our family. We always looked forward to enjoying the festive season with our maternal grandparents. I have so many amazing memories of waking up to stockings bursting with pressies, and running down the stairs with the dog to see the dazzling, ginormous tree towering over mounds of wrapped gifts. We'd have crackers at the dinner table, roast dinner and always, always a game of monopoly before bedtime.

On paper my maternal grandparents were Church of England. Although they never talked about religion, they always celebrated Christmas and other big events. Even at Easter, every year my grandad arranged egg hunts for us. I'm feeling so much nostalgia just sitting here writing about it!

It's funny, I have fonder memories of Christmas than I do of Eid – mainly because of the magical atmosphere that there is around Christmas time in Britain. I really consider myself to be one of the lucky ones. Some Muslims say it's not 'allowed' to mark Christmas, but I believe it's a vital part of the national British culture, and therefore it is a part of me, too. I am so happy that I got to experience

a harmony of different cultures and traditions in my life. I feel a little sad that my own kids won't have exactly the same experiences, but we all have our own different, unique lives and they get to experience another mixture of cultures. All I can say, is that I'm just so grateful for mine – it's shaped my life and who I am now. But let's rewind to when I was eleven years old. After five years of being settled in London, my parents decided to move to Wales. Yep, there's been a lot of moving in my life! But to be honest, I've never minded it. We went to Cairo every summer for two months, so I've always felt like I have more than one home, and here was another to add to the collection!

My dad had visited Cardiff for an exhibition, as he was trading in Egyptian souvenirs at the time. Basically, he quite liked the city – well, actually he REALLY liked it – so we all prepared for the next phase of our life.

It happened pretty fast. We relocated during half term, and it took my parents a few weeks to find a suitable school for all of us. When my sister and I finally joined our secondary school, bang in the middle of term, we were each paraded at the front of class for everyone to gawk at and welcome as 'the new kids'. This was done separately again, of course – God forbid you keep twins together, or else they'll never learn to make friends or know how to cope in the world!

We had been at an all-girl's school in London for the first half of the year, but our new school was co-ed. I spent the rest of Year 7 trying to make friends and figure out this whole new playing field. Suddenly there was such a thing as a 'bad boy', schoolkids having 'fags', a whole crowd of 'chavs' and gangs of pretty, popular girls ruling the roost! It was a far cry from what I had imagined school to be like in

Wales. I thought we'd be surrounded by rolling countryside, that there'd be super-strict teachers and that we'd be the only only Muslim kids in the whole school. None of that happened. Our new Welsh school was incredibly diverse; there were plenty of Muslims, Hindus, Christians and kids of all other faiths. It catered to pupils who spoke English as a second language and also excelled in supporting kids who were asylum seekers as well as refugees.

Overall, when I look back at the time I had there, I loved it! Of course, there were ups and downs that I'll get into later, but in general I was happy, especially once I'd found my group of friends. It was like United Colours of Benetton. There were six of us: me and my sis; Katie, the blonde-haired Welsh lass from the valleys; Aisha and Adeeba, the Pakistanis; and Desiree, who moved to London from Zimbabwe. Despite our diversity (which is, of course, on trend now), we weren't considered one of the popular 'cool' groups. In fact, we were always known as the 'laughing like a pack of hyenas' group. Very flattering! But we didn't care, as we had a great time together and, as you might have guessed, were always having fun. Without my close circle of friends, I know that high school could have been an absolute misery for me.

THE HIJAB YEARS

'She understood that the hardest times in life to go through were when you were transitioning from one version of yourself to another.'

Sarah Addison Allen

FIRST BLOOD

No sooner had I adjusted to the change of home, school environment and my circle of friends than I experienced another, more intimate, change.

I was eleven years old and I'd just got my bloody period – if you'll pardon the pun. When I told my mum that I'd need to start wearing some of her big ugly pads, she beamed at me, gave me a huge hug and assured me not to worry about a thing. I can't say I remember being worried, if I'm honest I was more pissed off than anything. You see, I was a proper little tomboy with a carefree attitude; I enjoyed my sports and just really enjoyed being a kid. So the thought of having to experience something that suddenly made me more 'girly' was a bit of a nuisance.

At that time, I really couldn't have cared less about how I looked. The majority of my wardrobe was from the boys' section at GAP – I used to wear nothing but combat shorts and oversized hoodies. I'd always have my hair in a ponytail, with the most embarrassing centre parting and a fringe that fell over my bushy brows. But now I'd started my period, I also started wearing a hijab – which saved everyone from that infamous centre parting!

JUST A PIECE
OF FABRIC?

My first day of wearing the hijab or a headscarf was also the first day back at school after the summer holidays. Lucky me! As I walked through the school gates, I'll be honest with you, I was shitting myself. It didn't help that my twin sister wasn't wearing a headscarf and that her hair was styled gorgeously into two braided bunches. Up until now, we'd always been pretty equal in everything we did, without competition. We even shared a circle of friends. But things had suddenly changed. She automatically became cooler and more accepted by the skaters and moshers. I felt very much like the 'loser' twin, which was a real shock and it changed how I saw myself.

When I decided to start wearing the hijab, I was physically transitioning. I developed body image issues, seeing myself as overweight and chubby. I lost my confidence and let my insecurities take over.

I hadn't anticipated how a simple change of look would become such a challenge for me, mainly because all these body issues that were thrown in the mix. At the time, I wasn't scared about wearing a hijab. To me, it wasn't such a big deal. I was always taught that you wear the hijab when you get your period, so it was a natural progression and an accepted part of my life. But I didn't let myself progress in other ways.

It can be tough. If you think being a young Muslim in today's society is hard, then try being a young Muslim girl in a hijab – there's no hiding away on a bad day for us! I give props to Muslim girls and women, especially those who are having a hard time wearing the hijab but are still committed to it.

It's not often that we get acknowledged for our daily struggles. I'd dare any of the men in our families and communities to walk a day in our shoes. I doubt they'd last one minute! If there are any men reading this, I say this: a little appreciation can go a long way. It's the Muslim women in hijab who largely end up taking the brunt of Islamophobia in our day-to-day lives. It is women in hijab struggling to fit in at work, at school, who are being told we shouldn't do this or that because we wear it. I so wish our generation were better informed about the hijab and that we could have challenged the many misconceptions about Islam that we all grew up with. Maybe then we wouldn't hold ourselves back so much, like I did.

Deep down, and what I came to truly understand later in life, is that commitment to wearing the headscarf should never stop you from living your life. I know this is easier said than done and the reality is that for some, that's not the case. I tried to see it as a beautiful, liberating practice that would allow me to shine in my abilities and my personality, and be acknowledged by the world for who I truly was and not by the way I looked. I didn't want to be judged on my appearance and conform to societys sexualisation of women (simply for just being a woman). My wearing of the hijab was like shouting out to the world, 'I am a Muslim and a proud one, too!'. We were very much unapologetically Muslim back then. It was (and still is) a huge part of our identity and something to feel proud of.

LOW POINTS
AND HIGH LESSONS

I absolutely loved sports when I was growing up and was always pretty active, but for some reason my athleticism went out of the window as soon as I started wearing a headscarf. I say 'for some reason' when, really, I know why. After years of not giving a flying F about my appearance, I suddenly became more conscious of how silly I'd look. I stopped playing football because I felt stupid being the only one in a hijab. I've always loved tennis and grew up playing it with my dad, but I stopped that, too. And I used to go horse riding every week, but I felt like an absolute loser in a scarf and a riding hat. No one was telling me this, it's just how I couldn't help but feel. I was the only one holding myself back.

I am sure, like a lot of girls, there were countless times during my teenage years that I'd cancel plans because I thought I looked fat in everything. I'd end up sobbing my eyes out into a heap of clothes that I thought didn't fit. Of course, hijab and the very essence of it is supposed to prevent this kind of complex, but in reality, every young girl will go through body image issues – and Muslim hijabis are certainly no exception. We'd be naïve to think that just because a girl is wearing a hijab that she automatically doesn't care about her appearance and is spiritually mature enough not to fall prey to the superficial pressures of society. Social media is so prevalent in shaping our youth these days, yet many people assume these girls are immune to its pressures, and so we're left with a community that's in denial and doesn't understand the everyday issues that our girls face.

In reality, the hijab shouldn't limit you in anything that you want to do. If only I'd had my current mentality of not putting so much pressure and stringency on wearing the headscarf then maybe I'd be a different person altogether now.

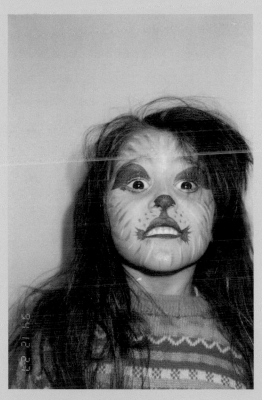

Looking back I realise how much of a mammoth decision it is for young girls to commit to wearing a headscarf at a young age. However, I believe that everything happens for a reason and in my case I'm glad of my experiences, as they have allowed me to delve deeper into what modestly and the hijab actually is and to gain my own understanding rather than buy into what we're systematically taught on a very general basis. Like: 'You must cover up to protect yourself from men, so they don't fancy you,' or, 'You're like an expensive diamond, and we keep expensive things safe' and more BS like that.

For example, I remember when I was about twelve years old, there was an image going around of two lollipops – one had a wrapper on it and the other was unwrapped and had dead flies on it. It told young women to hide their beauty or we'd end up with dead flies on us, which is absurd! But that's what we were exposed to. So many things in religion have been manipulated in favour of men, but what God would allow women to be treated unfairly? If we are Muslims and we are taught that He is the most merciful, then He wouldn't be unjust to women. Men's modesty in religion is as important as women's – the Quran addresses men's modesty first, then women's. We need to look into what our faith actually teaches, never follow it blindly or stupidly, like that lollipop picture!

My relationship with wearing the headscarf is ever fluctuating, with plenty of ups and downs over the almost twenty years of daily commitment. It will always be ingrained as part of my culture.

Modesty as a whole is something I think I will always try my best to adhere to as a general dressing guideline, it's just how I feel comfortable living my life, headscarf or not. I think it's so important for

girls to learn about hijab and what it means truly in a way that's grounded, balanced and also practical to their roles in society, rather than out of fear of 'going to hell'. So many tenets of Islam are taught to kids by instilling a fear in them – a fear of going to hell, a fear of God being angry – so kids are scared of the consequences rather than enjoying their religion. Kids shouldn't be brought up on fear and pressure of community judgement, they should be nurtured with love and choice instead; all these experiences can have an impact on their behaviour and attitude later on in life, so isn't it better to focus on the positive ones? This mentality and harsh approach to a religion that is so incredibly beautiful can suddenly turn people ugly at the pettiest of 'sins'.

HIJAB: MEANING

hijab

hɪˈdʒɑːb/

noun

noun: *hijab*; plural noun: *hijabs*

1   Dictionary definition: *a head covering worn in public by some Muslim women.*
    — the religious code which governs the wearing of the hijab.

2   Dina's definition: *basically, a piece of fabric that nowadays seems to end up determining how religious you MUST be in the eyes of everyone else!*

It's time to tackle hijab head on: what exactly is the hijab and modesty anyway?

When you think of a Muslim woman in hijab, there is almost always one picture that pops into most people's heads. But there shouldn't be, because the truth is this: the diversity is huge and colourful and, most importantly, authentic to each woman. We don't all wear black abayas and we don't all tie our scarves the same. There's no one way to do it, and there's definitely no one way to define being a Muslim woman.

Hijab itself is an Arabic noun. The literal definition is 'partition', 'separation' or 'barrier'. Many Muslims and non-Muslims mistake this word as the definition of a head covering. This is mainly because the word hijab has popularly come to refer to the headscarf that many muslim women wear, however, here common parlance rules over technicality!

The requirements of dressing modestly are debated amongst many Muslims globally, so I'm going to share what I've personally been taught growing up and what my take is. I was told the only parts that should be visible when in public are your face, your hands and your feet, leaving the rest of the body pretty much covered. Whilst there was a general influence on how to cover up from some countries in the Middle East (traditional black abaya – an easy option that suited the climate and environment), it was more or less open to interpretation for me.

A person's own understanding of the religious guidelines on wearing the hijab influences the style that is adopted. The styles

*'For many,
the hijab represents
modesty, piety and
devotion to God, and
I truly respect that.
But the hijab should
not be used as a
means of applying
social pressure
on people.'*

Queen Rania of Jordan

we wear are heavily influenced by our culture and surroundings. My way of dressing modestly is definitely reflective of the British Muslim experience. It's all about perspective. I believe clothing from any culture can be worn within the religious requirements of modest dressing, it's simply about how you wear clothes.

I'm still expanding my knowledge and viewpoint on wearing the headscarf in today's society, not just the idea of dressing modestly. I should add here that modest clothing is not something that's only reserved for Muslim women, or women of any faith for that matter, it's simply a path of conscious style that anyone can choose to follow. The same goes for wearing the headscarf. Whilst it is mainly Muslim women who are recognised for it, there are also women of other faiths who do this too. In fact, hijab is open to any female who chooses to wear it.

But for me as a Muslim woman, the physical aspect of dressing modestly should also reflect the inner aspect. Every time I step out into a public space, whether I like it or not, I'm a visual representation of Islam because of my headscarf. Being mindful of how we treat people including general members of the public, and all that other good behaviour stuff, should always be put into practice. What I'm trying to say is, basically, just be nice!

Now, by no means is my interpretation the 'only and correct' one. However, it will resonate with plenty of my fellow British Muslim hijabis. Wearing the hijab and incorporating the idea of modesty in our day-to-day lives can also act as a form of expression. It shouts to the world 'Hey, I'm a Muslim woman! This is how I choose to dress and this is how I identify myself.'

BRANDS AND HIJABS

It's great to see big brands using hijabis in their marketing, but I still question the integrity of their representation. Most of the time you can suss out when the collaboration is genuine or just token. A big sports brand contacted me about their new hijab. They know that the Muslim bloggers they reached out to already wear their brand but they only seem to want to be inclusive when it's to do with hijab,

not when it's about sportswear and trainers. So how inclusive are they being really? They're not including us in mainstream clothing and footwear, we are only approached when it comes to the hijab, because hijab means tick-box business.

A sports hijab is nothing I haven't seen before. I saw sportswear for Muslim women in Egyptian markets everywhere while growing up, but it's not 'cool' until it has a mainstream label on it. It's the same when a big brand does a 'Ramadan Collection'. All they've really done is use existing products and stuck a Ramadan label on it to cash in. This is just lazy. Muslim women are wearing brands all year round, so if these companies really want to champion inclusion, don't turn us into a trend. We aren't just about Ramadan or Eid, or even merely a sports hijab.

THE SHAPE OF ME

Who knew that getting dressed in a uniform every day would be such a huge problem? There were two types of trousers for school uniforms: the sexy lycra ones that all the cool girls would wear, and the baggy chino-style ones that all the losers wore. I was the latter, obviously.

I *hated* the shape of my butt. I always tried to pull my T-shirt over it. Since the T-shirts were always short-sleeved, we'd have to layer a long-sleeved top underneath to cover our arms, which in my mind just made me look extra fat. It was always a mission perfecting my scarf every morning, too, especially the bit by the collar; my scarf and collar always collided like rivals and resulted in a messy clash. Back then turban styles were not considered cool, and there certainly weren't any bloggers around to get inspo from!

So one of the hijab styles I wore consisted of shiny black lycra that was super snug around the neck. It used to push my chubby cheeks out from the sides of my scarf, so I always imagined that I looked like a big black flea. Oh gosh, for us young hijabis, cheeks were the bane of our lives! We'd constantly try different ways to hide them or 'tuck' them into our scarves. That goes for double chins, too. But doing this had its consequences – I used to pin my scarf so tightly that the safety pin would dig into me, leaving endless scabs. It even left a scar for a good few years! I pinned it tightly out of fear that some know-it-all, tit-face bully might pull it off my head. And of course, that fear was a reality and didn't sprout out of nowhere...

I was bullied during high school – although I didn't realise it was bullying then. I never thought it was serious at the time, but having said that, we should never take any form of bullying lightly. I was lucky I didn't let it get to me, and that's thanks to my mama, who made sure we knew how to stick up for ourselves with our words rather than with our fists.

And boy was I a loud mouth! I was quick to make a bully look silly, but sometimes that didn't always work in my favour. There was this one specific guy who sticks out in my memory who was also, incidentally, a Muslim. He had a sister a year or two above us who also wore a headscarf, as did his mum, but for some idiotic reason, he found it amusing to belittle me in front of our classmates for wearing one myself. He'd constantly tug at the back of my scarf, make rude comments and call me strange names like 'donkey'. This happened on a daily basis for the majority of my high school years. Thank goodness I didn't let it bother me, otherwise I don't know how I would feel about my school experiences now.

THE TEENAGE YEARS

Teenage years can be the best time for some, but for others… not so much. You can worry about the most random, silly and pointless things most of the time. To illustrate this, here are some disjointed thoughts from a fifteen-year-old Dina:

'I hope Mrs Jones forgets about English homework today, cuz I have. My scarf is just not behaving today. Life would be so much easier if I could show my hair. I bet then I'd be considered one of the pretty girls. All the boys would be after me then, hmph! I wonder if my arch enemy is going to try pulling my scarf off in class today? Maybe I should put in a few extra pins to make sure he can't. I should probably start revision for mock exams, but what's the point of all this stress if they aren't even REAL exams??? And what the hell is that minging spot on my chin, I'd better pop it. Hope no one notices the Primark tag on my jacket today, that's the last thing I need.'

See? Pointless! Although I'm sure a lot of you recognise and empathise with these thoughts! When I think back to my high-school years, I have both fond, fun, as well as some cringeworthy and painful memories. It's important to have a solid circle of friends to get through high school – I know it was the one thing that helped me conquer it. It didn't matter that we weren't considered the 'popular' ones. Even when we'd get picked on by the admired A-list 'mean girls' of our time, it didn't matter, because inside our circle, we knew we were all funny as hell and cooler than a cucumber.

I know it's easier said than done – finding friends, that is – especially if socialising doesn't come as easy to you, but it makes all the difference having one close friend you can rely on. Someone who can be your go-to partner for a class project and someone to have constant banter with. If you find that someone, you'll have each other's backs no matter what.

But despite having a solid circle of friends, and a great family around me, it still didn't save me from the most serious phase I went through: having an eating disorder.

EATING DISORDER

I was around fifteen years old when I started developing a strange relationship with food. I couldn't pinpoint the reasons for this – I don't think it was because of the bullying, and it wasn't because of loneliness. But I did believe I was fat. I was constantly trying to lose weight and achieve the 'perfect' figure. I became obsessive about calorie counting and working out. By working out, I mean riding an exercise bike in the attic for three hours straight before going to sleep. And then, before bedtime, I would binge. I'd have five slices of toast piled with butter, followed by consuming ALL the KitKats in the cupboard as well as finishing all the leftovers in the fridge. If I was going to eat, I was going to EAT.

My mum noticed that I ate a lot, but then she thought we all ate like crazy. Remember, I had two brothers and a sister eating the house out too, so my overeating got obscured. I also hid the fact that I binged. My family saw me eating dinner, but when everyone was upstairs, I'd sneak down to the kitchen, hide food under my jumper and tiptoe back upstairs to eat in secret. Even when I ate crisps in front of them, I'd sneakily empty three packets into one, then eat them in the living room.

Food was taking over my life. It was consuming my brain. The only thing I ever thought about was what I was going to eat next. I didn't care how much I ate because I thought I'd just exercise it off all in one go or starve the next day, then binge all over again. That was my mentality! Exercise bulimia is the correct term for it, I believe. I'd eat and eat until I was unable to move. This went on for years, about seven I would say. That's a long time to do that to myself.

It then morphed into something even more harmful – 'shitting bulimia', if I was to give it a

name. Instead of exercising like a madwoman to get rid of the calories I'd binged earlier, I'd poo it all out with the help of laxatives. At first I was just using them as advised on the packet, 1–2 tablets after food. Then I started thinking, the more laxatives I take, the more I can poo. I ended up taking a whopping forty laxative pills a day, which meant being stuck on the toilet for most of the night. This happened for a good three years of my life. Looking back, I can't believe what extreme measures I took. And the ironic, and really stupid, thing is that I didn't lose any weight at all!

I was actually quite open about all this with my family – well, to a certain extent. They knew I was weird with food, but they thought I was taking laxatives because of constipation. They had no clue just how many I was taking. My mum would voice her concerns and talk to me regularly about it, but I always made out like it wasn't really a big deal, probably because at the time I didn't realise how serious it was. And if I didn't confront it as a problem, there wasn't anything my family could do. I needed to face up to the issue and help myself – unfortunately I didn't do this for a while.

Of course, it was the worst thing I could do to my body. I'd get really bad pains in my chest and cramps in my stomach. It's a miracle I wasn't more seriously affected, and the only reason I stopped was by chance. I had a weekend job at Primark, and I picked up a magazine on my lunch break. In it was an interview with an *EastEnders* actress who talked about her eating disorder. It was the exact same thing I was going through, but she ended up in hospital with heart problems from a laxative overdose. It was a massive wake-up call for me. From that moment, I realised what I was doing to my body and decided it had to stop. I weaned myself

off the laxatives by using herbal alternatives instead and I managed to save myself.

I have since realised that I picked up this laxative idea from Egyptian social culture. There's a laxative tea that many Arab women have after big meals. I remember them sipping on it and laughing about needing to shed the food we had just stuffed our faces with. And so naturally us young girls followed suit. It's no wonder I didn't realise how serious my 'addiction' was, as it seemed to be the usual attitude towards food and dieting in a culture that I was exposed to. When talking about this in recent years, I've come to learn that it's a wider problem within the Muslim community, and one that needs professional help. We have to make it obvious to people how detrimental the habit is.

Also, something we don't realise is that Muslims who suffer from these disorders can feel alone and really struggle in Ramadan. All the people I know who are battling eating disorders have a big relapse during Ramadan. My question is, should they even be fasting? Eating disorders are a mental health issue, and people can become seriously ill. That's not what fasting is about. If they are bingeing on iftar and then throwing it all up or, as in my case, shitting it all out, then we have to talk about it and support them. I can't believe that eating disorders affect up to around 700,000 people in the UK alone. I've been just one of that number, and it all stemmed from anxiety around my body image issues. So many young people suffer from some form of anxiety, and that anxiety can trigger so many other problems, which brings me to another disorder…

HAIR PULLING

'To lose confidence in one's body is to lose confidence in oneself.'

Simone de Beauvoir

During my weird eating years I was also addicted to hair pulling and, like my eating problems, I was oblivious that this was even a big issue. I later realised that I was in fact suffering from trichotillomania – a disorder that results in an irresistible urge to pull out hair.

Every evening after school, I'd sit there watching TV while pulling out one hair after the other. It was always the same spot that I used to pull and all I remember is how satisfying it felt. And it got worse. I also moved on to pulling out my eyebrow and eyelash hairs. It was a terrible addiction, an outlet for the anxiety I didn't even realise I had. The hair pulling went on for years, until one day, while playing around with my hair in front of the mirror, I gasped when I saw a bald spot that I had created. I was absolutely mortified! Seeing that bald patch was the kick I needed to break the awful habit. I took hair-growing pills (bought from a reputable company – never buy from a random site on the internet, do your research!) and thankfully I managed to stop doing that to myself.

Young people, especially girls, go through so much and often it's not taken seriously enough. There's a whole load of problems that are triggered by our insecurities and anxieties. If I could go back in time, I'd tell myself DON'T DO IT, YOU'LL LOSE YOUR HAIR! I managed to control it, but for so many young girls it's far worse and they cannot stop. If you're like me, and don't even realise how serious the addiction is, it can be very dangerous. I hope that anyone reading about my experience will recognise the problem and get help. Tell someone you trust. A relative perhaps, or it might even be easier to tell a stranger, or a school counsellor. There is always someone there to support you.

I had people around me – a stable family and good friends – but I still didn't tell anyone, I wish I had. Hair pulling, eating disorders, it can happen to any one of us, but don't let it make you suffer. You are your only saviour.

ONLINE PRESSURE

The social media world has ballooned since the time I was at school. We only had hi5, Myspace and MSN Messenger back then, which sounds a bit sad, but in some ways, I think it made school life a little bit easier.

We wouldn't be glued to our phones 24 / 7 for one thing, although as soon as we got home from school, we'd get on the computer or laptop. It was like an extension of social life in school, but everyone seemed a lot bolder online: there they projected their alter egos.

I didn't succumb to this, although I have to say that peer pressure can be very powerful. Thankfully I was less easily influenced by what was around me and was happy to do my own thing, while disagreeing loudly with other people. My mum always taught us 'it's okay to say no' and I'd basically say no all the time to everyone, teachers included! (Although I don't actually always recommend this...!)

My time on the internet was limited, thanks to my parents. They'd give me half an hour on the computer and that was it. They'd always ask me what I was doing online and to whom I was talking. I'm actually glad they were on the ball about social media at the time. As young teens, we only see the fun and it's easy to get sucked in. We can't see the potential dangers.

There are so many horrific cases of bullying and blackmail online and parents are often completely oblivious. I've seen Instagram pages belonging to eleven-year-olds who look a whole lot older in the pictures they're posting. How does that not ring alarm bells for parents? We need to make our kids aware of the dangers and the emotional effects that social media and online pressures can have.

My parents (Mum especially) taught me what the boundaries were when I went online. They taught me what not to do and what to do. This prepared me for when I was allowed to get my first, very own laptop. I felt so grown up! It's important that internet dos and don'ts are taught and supported in education and not just at home – protection and prevention are key.

COLLEGE YEARS, CARS AND CONFIDENCE

'Confidence is a journey – not a destination.'

Tess Holliday

When high school is over and you've just about managed the hurdle of GCSEs you then have your next decision to make: go to college, or stay in school to attend Sixth Form. The cool thing to do was set off to a different college, which is what my sister ended up doing. But I decided to stick to what I knew best and stay in the same place. Our friends' circle split in the same way, with one half staying and the other half leaving for college. This meant my circle suddenly became much smaller. Maybe it was the fact that we were such a small group that all of a sudden I fitted in more. Or maybe it was down to growing up a little and knowing myself better.

I was seventeen. I'd lost weight and had become more comfortable in my skin. I became more stylish with my headscarf and outfits, and I became more confident. With confidence came my personality. I slowly became the joker of the pack, and I loved making everyone laugh. I was popular with the teachers (or at least I liked to think so) and I was convinced I was the bees knees! Even boys started showing a little interest. I could tell some of the Muslim male friends in our group quite liked me, although they never said anything and nothing ever came of it. But it gave me a little boost to get the attention, especially thinking back to what I was only a couple of years earlier – a girl with absolutely no confidence at all.

Another big boost came from having some responsibility: our school opened up job positions to sixth formers during the lunch hour. I applied with a friend and we got the job. We had to organise the lunch hall and hand out dinner cards to the younger years. We quickly earned respect from the kids. They'd come to us for advice on boys, girls, homework, or even family problems. I loved to help them out

in any way I could. As well as earning money,
I finally felt I was starting to find my feet.

Then came the next big chapter – getting
my driving licence! My sister and I both passed
our tests at the same time, and together we bought
a little Peugeot 206. We were among the first in our
group of friends to get both a licence and a car, so
instantly we became HOT hijabis! Ha! I used to
cruise around for hours with my seat reclined,
my hijab flying out of the window and the music
blasting out. I'd even bop my head to the beat with
one hand on the wheel and the other hanging out
the window. I'm cringing just thinking about it!
I'd give everyone lifts to college and Sixth Form,
then go to see my sister and her new friends.
Slowly but surely, our circle of mates became
pretty big.

During all of this, I developed my
own style. I used to collect bandanas in
different colours and wear them as the front
peak in my hijab style. I ended up with a
pretty decent collection and some of the
younger girls in the year below would start
styling theirs in the same way! If I was going
somewhere fancy, I'd stick a bling diamante
brooch on the side. I thought I was so fly.
Ugh. Style takes time to grow, I guess.
I had to start somewhere!

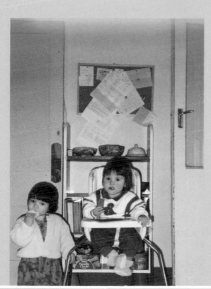

CONFUSED.COM

One of the routes that later led me into fashion was doing Textiles as a GCSE. I did pretty well, so my plan was to continue it at A level and eventually become a designer. But it wasn't as easy during A levels. I found it hard to concentrate. I was more interested in hanging out with mates and soaking up that newfound attention! I fell behind quickly and although I managed to scrape some grades together, they nowhere near reflected my potential. When everyone else started to think about their careers and university, I was a little lost. I had enjoyed my English Literature A level, but not to the extent of wanting to pursue it further. I was sure I enjoyed fashion and designing clothes, but realistically, was I ever really going to make a career out of it? I'd never heard of blogging before, and wasn't aware of any hijabi designers in the fashion industry. I thought I wouldn't fit in, that I'd be the only visibly Muslim girl on the course and it would be a waste of time and money. I quickly dismissed it as an option. With all my doubt, I pushed back applying to uni until the very last minute. I ended up getting onto the most random course: Psychology.

Let's just say I had a big fat reality check when I went to university. It was a far cry from anything like Sixth Form. We were certainly not spoon-fed and I guess I just wasn't ready for the independence that we were suddenly propelled into. I think when you're eighteen, you're either really ready for university or you're way too immature to stick it out. I couldn't even figure out how to get to my lectures, let alone listen to them. I had no idea what I was doing. The course was way over my head.

Having never studied psychology before, to being thrown into a sink-or-swim situation, I felt overwhelmed and decided to give up. That's when I got my first call-centre job. I stayed there for a good year NOT saving, unlike most 'gap year' students would do! I pretty much spent my entire pay cheque on a spanking new Vauxhall Corsa, which I bought on finance. I had no clue what I was going to do for my career. Even in this call-centre job, I avoided calls! I decided to quit before getting sacked, and managed to get myself a decent reference. By that time, university applications had started again, so I thought I'd give it another go, this time applying for something I was interested in… kind of…

Religious and Theological Studies.

WHAT?

I know, SO random.

I think you're getting my pattern now. Although I lasted a full year, when the second year came around, I couldn't be bothered to go in. So, on my first day back, I decided to quit. Again. No surprises there then. I started work in another call centre, helping old people renew their Sky TV packages all day. That was followed by joining yet another call centre, this time helping old people fix their electrical goods from Tesco over the phone. Oh, the joy. Don't get me wrong, it's perfectly fine to work in a call centre, but I was just passing time again, avoiding calls and pranking customers. There was one specific game that we used to play when a customer was too much hassle. We would pick a word or even a phrase and stick it into the conversation as many times as possible without the customer noticing, I would be in fits of laughter by the time I'd hung up. I was the work clown and I had zero ambition. I basically wasted three years of my life.

FINDING YOUR FEET: DINA'S TWO-PENCE WORTH

A LEVELS

Choosing A levels is possibly the biggest decision of your life at age sixteen, and the pressure is really on to figure everything out at that time. Your whole life seems to rely on three or four subjects that you have to commit yourself to for the next few years. I'd say the best way to look at it is to think about what subjects you truly find interesting and can imagine writing pages and pages about. If you get a feeling of 'heavy chest', as I like to call it (basically a feeling of dread), then steer away! But in all honesty, it's never too late to delve into new territory later on if you're not quite sure what you want to do yet.

If you are confused, I suggest you consult your parents, because they only want what's best for you. But if you're utterly sure it's a subject path you really don't want to take, then it's okay to disagree with them too. Be firm but polite. Sometimes parents get panicky when you haven't figured out your future yet at exam stage, and they automatically try to take control, but if there's one thing I've learnt from my experience, it's the importance of persistence. I always managed to win them round when I was persistent with decisions, proving to them that I knew what I wanted and that I was going to work hard for it. That's all they want really – for you to have passion and drive.

MOTIVATION
VS
PROCRASTINATION

Procrastination. I remember the first time I heard that word I had to look it up. It's a word lots of teens use to describe their weekend just before exam week. It's so hard to get motivated, even now as an adult sometimes I get stuck in a rut. But I use these five top tips to help kickstart that much-needed self-motivation.

1   Be realistic. Don't leave things to the last minute, because even if you complete it on time, it won't be to your standard. So set yourself a realistic target or goal that isn't overwhelming. This way you don't end up rushing and being disappointed with the outcome.

2   When in doubt, reflect on your past achievements. Remind yourself that you are talented and you CAN do the next task. More importantly, YOU WILL.

3   Surround yourself with fellow people 'who get shit done'. That leaves less room for wasting time and more room for supporting each other. In other words, the influence of productivity is key.

4   Similar to Tip 1, avoid putting too much pressure on yourself. Procrastination is a result of lots of pressure building up which finally combusts in a 'I give up' attitude.

5   Don't compare what you've achieved so far to what anyone else has done. You may end up feeling out of your depth and defeated. Your successes are your unique successes – value them and own them.

CHOOSING YOUR CAREER

For those who want to be a doctor, engineer, dentist or teacher, you pretty much know what steps you need to take to get there. For others who want to get into a more creative career, you don't necessarily need to rely on a university degree, although it certainly will help. Your portfolio and work experience is *the* most important thing when it comes to pursuing a career in the creative zone. Many people are taking the initiative to self-train – going on the necessary programmes and courses to become experts. It's also important to remember that nothing comes easily. There may be some steps you won't enjoy but that you have to take in order to achieve your goals. Ultimately, hard work, determination and a splash of competitiveness will get you where you want to be, whatever path you end up choosing.

The ideal is that your work shouldn't feel like a job. Do something you have a clear passion for, something that fulfils you and something you can imagine having a long-standing career in. If, like me, you are unsure as to what your future holds, it's probably handy to ask yourself a few questions to figure out what kind of personality you are:

— *Are you a people person and do you like socialising?*

— *What kind of character do you have? Or what would you say are your key character traits?*

— *What are your hobbies or past times?*

— *What five things are you talented in?*

— *Do you enjoy practical activities or are you more of a bookworm?*

— *Are you the kind of person who likes to be settled or do you love a bit of spontaneity?*

Gather up all your answers and think of the kind of career that complements them or the type of work that would suit you – an office job, working with customers or in small creative teams? There will probably be a few possible outcomes, but the goal would be to find something that revolves around your interests as well as your talents. In addition to loving our jobs, it's also vital that we flourish in them!

SID

It was Sid who helped me to move on from working in a call centre. Sid and I met on Facebook, as much as it pains me to say it. I got a message one day from a 'Sid Kaan' with a simple 'Hey'.

Of course, I fully stalked his profile before messaging back with a 'Who's this?'. I pretended I may have known him from somewhere, when really I just thought he was pretty hot. The conversation got started and I won't go into too much detail because, frankly, it's too embarrassing to repeat. Just imagine a long thread of cringeworthy messages to and fro – me playing the hard-to-get card with a bunch of 'gangsta' phrases and Sid pretty much asking me out for 'tea' every five minutes. This went on for about two months until we finally decided to meet, with the purpose of him giving me an application form for Tesco, where he then worked.

The first time we actually met was at the traffic lights, which I guess was symbolic as things were about to change! The first thought that popped into my head when I saw Sid was, 'Where's the rest of him?!' He was a lot shorter than I expected. I only had Facebook photos to go on, and we know how reliable they can be sometimes. I had already built a persona around him in my head to be a tall basketball player who was super cool but had a hint of dorky charm about him. Sid was dressed in an oversized T-shirt and crazily baggy jeans with huge embroidered wings on the back. It's safe to say I was ecstatic to see them get binned later on! After he gave me the application form, we sort of slyly checked each other out, both feeling the awkwardness of the situation. We walked around the town centre making small talk. We stayed in touch, chatting to each other every day for the next few weeks. I eventually got that job at Tesco too!

'All too often people concentrate on finding the right spouse, little realizing that half of any marriage is being the right spouse.'

Yasir Qadhi

We weren't on the same team but we'd always meet for breaks and lunch. Despite seeing each other almost every day, we were yet to admit what was really going on with our feelings – both to ourselves and to each other.

One day, Sid invited me to his sister's wedding party and of course I couldn't wait to go. Sid is Pakistani and I loved Asian culture. The music, the clothes, the food – I found it all so fun and vibrant, so any chance for me to go to town in my outfit was a no-brainer. It was the first time Sid saw me dressed up and vice versa. It was also the first time for me to meet all his family at once. But I wasn't scared about it because in my head we were 'just friends', right?

WRONG.

That same night, once the party was over and we had all gone home, I was, of course, on the phone to Sid. While we were speaking, his sister casually asked him if he wanted to get to know one of her friends. Sid's reply to his sister was a flat 'No'. She then proceeded to ask if it was because he was with me. To my surprise he snapped back, 'Yes, Dina's my girlfriend!' Let me tell you, it was news to me, mate! But for some reason I didn't protest and that's pretty much how we made it 'official'! From that moment on, we decided to do things properly and tell our parents. If you're a Muslim reading this, then you understand how daunting it is to tell your parents that you've found the one you want to spend the rest of your life with. Actually, it's a scary thought for anyone, regardless of your religious background! It's got to be something to do with the L word (love), which might lead you on to thinking about the S word (sex).

Once we had decided to be together and make things official, it took us quite some time to get our parents to take our marriage requests seriously.

Well, it was mainly my dad making excuses as to why he wasn't ready to meet Sid as a serious contender for marriage. One of them was that Sid hadn't yet graduated from university. He was in his second year of studying motion graphic design at the time.

So we waited until his final year passed. But after that, Baba's next reason was that Sid needed to get his career sorted. There was a whole load of phone calls from Sid's dad to mine and a lot of back and forth until Dad finally agreed to meet Sid and his father. I was in Cairo when Sid and his father came over to see my dad for the very first meeting. I had gone to Egypt for a few months, because both Sid and I knew we were a distraction to each other. I'd gone to do some teaching and he in the meantime had got himself a full-time job. Although I wasn't there, my sister was on the phone to me the whole time giving me live updates. But even she wasn't in the room with them. If Sid were an Egyptian guy, and I was present, then we'd all have been in the same room having tea together and discussing the future, but my dad was being difficult.

Sid filled me in on how it went soon after – but it wasn't a good update. Basically, Baba's answer was a polite 'No'. Well, he didn't really say no, he just kept saying 'Dina's not ready yet'. He said we should wait a little longer. I can understand why; it was the first time they'd ever met and I think it was a lot for him to get his head around. His daughter wanted to get married, but he wasn't an Egyptian, or any other kind of Arab, he was a Pakistani. Dad was worried about a culture that was not in the slightest way similar to ours.

I felt this was hypocritical of my dad – I mean, he married a white Englishwoman! But his argument was that English culture is not as strong as Egyptian,

and it only works when one culture isn't dominant. He felt that the Pakistani culture was so strong, that it would overpower our Egyptian culture. I guess he did have a point, although I argued that Sid had been brought up in the UK. Baba took nearly four years to finally give his blessing, but it was also because I was too young. I would have been 21 if he had agreed straightaway, and to be honest, I would not have coped adjusting to married life at that age. I can guarantee that my Baba had emotional and protective feelings that any father would have for his daughter, he was just an overly worried parent, not the big mean stereotype of a Muslim dad that I'd painted him to be at the time. I'm now secretly glad he took four years to give us his blessing. So you could say it all worked out in the end.

The struggle that Sid and I went through actually helped to save our other siblings from a similar resistance from both sets of parents. My sister married a white Welsh guy, Sid's younger sister married a half-black, half-white guy, and his brother married a half-Arab, half-Welsh woman! So our breakthrough paid off for everyone!

I ended up getting married at twenty-four and Sid, twenty-seven. Even then I don't think I was ready. I don't think anyone's ever really ready. Especially if, like me, you had never lived with anyone other than your family before, never got intimate with a boyfriend before and never had to NOT rely on your mum's cooking and cleaning and waking you up for work!

DINATOKIO IS BORN

'People tend to believe that to be modern you have to disengage from your heritage, but it's not true.'

Sheikha Mozah bint Nasser

It was around 2010, during the back and forth period of trying to get married, that I started blogging. Well, technically it wasn't really blogging, more like Facebooking. It started with a small, second-hand sewing machine that I bought from a car boot sale in Cardiff. I'd sit at home on the floor, prop the sewing machine on some books and cut fabrics into shapes around my figure, then sew it all together. I didn't have books to teach me how to sew properly – I didn't have the patience to read through them to be honest – so it was all guesswork. My mum showed me how to do a bat-wing top, and I used that technique to make everything else.

I would style out my creations and get Sid to take pictures in the photography studio at his uni. I would then upload them onto my 'DINATOKIO' Facebook page to showcase my 'genius' work! I would go to work at Tesco in the evenings and make sure my colleagues were following my page and liking all of my pictures. Everyone was generally very supportive and loved it, I even had a few makeover requests from my fellow teammates! An hour after I posted, I got a hundred likes, a week later, I had a thousand. People from the mosque, school and work started to take notice and my Facebook page grew quickly.

I was constantly experimenting, and I was fearless. I didn't care if it was a crazy outfit, I became popular as my style was so different. Yet even when I first got into blogging, I still didn't think I would turn it into a career. I was still applying for fashion jobs and used blogging as my CV. It's funny how the brands I applied to back then are the very same brands who want to collaborate with me now!

A year after I began blogging, my Facebook audience encouraged me to get onto YouTube. I had only watched YouTube for cat videos up until this

point, but I began to take it more seriously. I researched to see who was out there on the Muslim social media scene. I found Amena, better known then as 'Pearl Daisy', who was one of the first British Muslim bloggers. And there was YaztheSpaz, the American Cuban-Turkish blogger. Both of them dressed in classic and traditional looks. It was great to see them online doing their thing, but I couldn't relate to it as much as I wanted to, as their style was individual to them and different to mine. It wasn't the urban, british vibe I wanted to capture, but they were clearly very popular with their audiences. The interest was clearly there, now there was space for more variety in the field!

So, in 2011, I started a YouTube channel, and then an actual blog. At first, I was a little hesitant. I felt like a right loser talking to my laptop camera; I would sit in my room and make sure everyone was out of the house before filming because I would get so embarrassed. I used to edit on the slowest movie maker ever on my laptop. It would take me hours, sometimes days, to edit even the simplest of videos! Plus it was all so low-budget and sparse – the only lighting came through the window.

In fact it's only recently that I started to get comfortable with the idea of being a full-time YouTuber. Yet even now if I'm vlogging and a group of girls walk past, I put the camera down as I get so self-conscious!

But I absolutely LOVE making videos, from the editing (even though sometimes that can be a nightmare) right through to reading all the comments on them. I used to reply to comments on Facebook, but I ended up stopping on YouTube as I wanted to appear a bit more professional. Now I've realised that engagement with your audience is important and something as small as leaving a reply can show your appreciation to them.

Some people have been critical, of course. Telling me I'm a bad Muslim, and this isn't how Muslims are meant to dress. Internet judgement is something I have definitely had to deal with. I remember not allowing it to get to me, as I already felt too much pressure about what I was putting out to worry about what was coming in. I had so much passion that I needed to get out of my system, and I think that passion saved me from getting affected by the negativity. I get that mental strength from my mum; we both have our own minds and are strong in our opinions. You don't mess with us!

I am also careful about how I manage social media. Many people might think I'm using it 24 / 7, but the truth is, I barely have my phone out. When I switch off, I switch off. I don't share too much personal stuff, either, but for some people it's more difficult; not only are they addicted, they can also be uber sensitive to nasty comments. I would suggest setting your boundaries: don't let it consume your real life when it's just an internet troll. It takes them a second to write it, but gives you hours of worrying. It's a shame we don't spend the same amount of time thinking about the positive

comments! So no, I've never been put off by the Haram Police. I never feel like giving up and I've always had something to share.

One of the best things anyone can derive from this line of work is the deep sense of satisfaction in creating something that is ALL you. It's your hard graft, your creativity. It's amazing to be able to present my channel to so many people globally and know that it's helped create awareness, and hopefully invited even the teeniest of smiles on someone's face. I am so grateful I've been able to share it all. So many people have grown with me over the last few years, watched me mature into an adult, watched me get married. You are the ones who have been with me, especially while I've been embracing motherhood in the messiest of ways! We're like a huge family. Sometimes we disagree on things, but ultimately my audience is like one big support network. It's actually incredible to think of the opportunities that social media has brought for me, as it has done for so many others.

BLOGGING: MY TOP TIPS

For the majority of my blogging life, I was doing it as a hobby. I wasn't making a penny for a very long time. Even my YouTube videos didn't garner any revenue when I first started – I didn't even know that was a thing back then. So, here are my top tips on how to turn your blogging hobby into a career.

STAY FOCUSED.

It's a challenge to stay motivated, especially when blogging could take ages to turn into something sustainable. You can lose focus, get distracted and even find it hard to blog at all. My tip is to take time out and change your environment when things get really busy. A break can give you space to breathe and that's when ideas grow. You can simply go into another room in the house, listen to music, look at books and magazines, walk in the countryside, or even go away for a weekend to visit family. When I do any one of these, I come back full of new ideas.

DON'T LOSE YOUR PASSION.

Sometimes when you turn what was once a hobby into work, it can be easy to lose the fun factor. All of a sudden, you've got deadlines to meet and guidelines to follow when you're working with brands as a content creator. The worst thing is when you start looking at it purely as work, because you'll lose what you were once passionate about. I find that I'm always reflecting and reminding myself why I started this in the first place, especially when the stress starts to creep in. The reason I started was a combination of frustration and passion, to be honest! I found that the representation of Muslim women out there was all negative or stereotypical. None of it related to me. I knew so many Muslim women like me who were cool,

trendy as hell and had a great life. So I went
online to represent me and my friends – to tell
our story for ourselves. I remind myself of this
from time to time, which keeps me reaching
high, because if you lose that passion, you
won't bring out quality content.

KEEP YOUR CONTENT ORIGINAL.

This is so so so important, especially now
when just about anybody can be a blogger.
If you want to have a long career and last as a
blogger you must stay original. I can't stress this
enough. Nearly a decade ago, when a bunch of
us started, we all had some kind of purpose and
message. That's always been my call; I base all
my content around that purpose. But the market
is saturated now, and many people do it for
a career change from a purely business angle.
Yet the profiles that have the best-quality content
are the ones that began with a reason. Plus they
are relatable. I share my life and personality,
and I'm interactive with my audience. It makes
a huge difference, trust me!

MAKE SURE YOU'RE IN
IT FOR THE RIGHT REASONS.

A lot of people look at bloggers and see this
perfectly curated image of a carefree life, full
of fun and luxury, and then they might want
to start blogging for the materialistic benefits.
Whilst blogging can definitely have some
amazing perks, if you're only starting because
you think you're going to get rich quick and get
shed loads of freebies, stop. If you want to show
the fame, also show the shit. Don't sell a fake
life to youth. It's the same with make-up, if I'm

going to do photos caked with make-up, I'll upload a picture of me without make-up so people know what I really look like. And importantly, don't even acknowledge you're not in make-up, just make it normal. There's nothing wrong with sharing a pretty photo, but selling this superficial fake lifestyle can be dangerous. I can't believe young people are getting fillers and Botox and cosmetic surgery. It's becoming so easy, and that's very scary, and all because they're chasing a snapshot dream on Instagram. It's important to show the real side. I'm just a regular person, with bills to pay, struggling in life like everyone else, and trying to raise kids. Us bloggers aren't celebrities, we're normal. And most bloggers work darn hard. The late nights and the forty-plus hours a week is the part you don't get to see. It can be difficult to find time off. Which brings me to my final tip…

TAKE TIME OFF.

When you start blogging, you're going to find that every minute of your day is based around your blogging work, which essentially means you don't really get any time off. At first you won't feel the need, but once your blogging gets going, ensure you allocate some social media free time during the week. It's so easy to get caught up in social media and blogging in a very unhealthy way, both mentally and physically, so it's incredibly important to unwind and take in real life, too.

*'God is
beautiful and loves
beauty.'*

Prophet Muhammad
(peace and blessings be upon him)

Fashion

INTRODUCTION TO MODEST FASHION

Let's face it, modest fashion has been around for centuries, but the term 'modest fashion' went mainstream when it was coined by big brands during recent years. The sudden drive to attract Muslim customers came from the realisation of global Muslim spending power on clothing and footwear: it was reportedly 266 billion dollars in 2013, according to Thomson Reuters and DinarStandard. And it's expanding at a massive rate, estimated to balloon to 484 billion dollars in 2019! So it's a no-brainer that major companies would seize the chance to reach out to Muslim audiences.

Muslim women have been shopping for modest clothing on the high street ever since I can remember. To me, modest fashion is a choice that takes a little more thought process to nail and one that requires a few more layers, with a bit more fabric! It's not solely for Muslim women or those in hijab either. Otherwise it should have been coined as 'Muslim fashion', right? It's understandable that it's been largely mistaken as something JUST for Muslim women, as the current market has been dominated by us. But in reality, it has much wider appeal. There's a huge community of Jewish, Christian, Hindu and Sikh women who also choose to opt for this style. If you want to call it 'faith-based fashion', I won't disagree, but it's important to mention that there are women of no faith who also choose to dress this way. Sometimes they may not even realise they'd fall under the modest fashion label! Simply put, modest fashion is for any woman who incorporates this choice as part of her lifestyle.

Right now, though, it's Muslim women that we are seeing in the fashion world. And that's largely due to social media. The hijabi blogosphere really took off in the last decade or so. It was impossible for mainstream brands to disregard their

popularity, reach and appeal. There have been collaborations with bloggers on campaigns, clothing lines, beauty products... the list goes on. It seems like this is a good thing, in the name of diversity and inclusion and all, although it can sometimes feel tokenistic or plain money making – but that's what businesses are all about.

However, I do think that big brands should also think about championing ethical values. If it truly is to be 'modest fashion', I don't think it should just focus on the clothing and the people who wear it. It should look at the whole process: the brand morals, integrity and fairness. Then it becomes so much more than just a garment.

Take a look at UNIQLO's partnering with the British-Japanese designer, Hana Tajima. That's a positive example of how it's done right. Hana Tajima has been a designer for the 'modest' audience for years and her work with UNIQLO was the perfect collaboration. You could see that the line was authentic to her and that's why it worked. It's clear there is mutual respect for each party and it comes across genuinely to the consumer.

We even saw hijabi models on major runways at New York Fashion Week. That's something I thought I would never see! But thanks to Halima Aden, there are now many girls following in her footsteps. It's a revolution for the modelling world. We now have models with a voice. Models who can don't need to compromise their beliefs and style choices if they want to work for huge brands. That in itself is amazing and really should be the right of every model, hijabi or not, don't you think?

When it comes to Muslims, modesty in general is about being humble, breaking egos and being genuine. If all this was applied to Muslim modest fashion we could provide a sincere, valuable

difference compared to what the mainstream are able to offer.

The key to successful representation is working with us and not just using us at the final stage as poster girls. How many of us are working with brands behind the scenes? How many of us are making decisions about how the public will perceive us? Only when we have been included in those higher positions on the projects that characterise OURSELVES, that is the point at which we know we've made a positive change, and that brands are truly diverse. That is true representation.

Whether Muslim women are used as a token or not, this is all part of the learning process. Remember, this is all still very new for us and for brands, so mistakes are inevitable. However, gradually and undeniably, progress is happening. For now, anything that normalises seeing and hearing diverse women on billboards and screens can only be a good thing. And the more of us that see relatable representations, the more of us will believe that we can do the same, and then we will see a ripple effect. Well, I hope so anyway!

HIJAB: STYLING

Wearing the headscarf and dressing modestly can be challenging. I remember when it was much more difficult to shop for a modest wardrobe than it is now. I had to make do with short dresses, as *actual* tops would never cover my butt. I also had to add plain long-sleeved tops as undertops to every 'main' top because the sleeves were never ever long enough. We'd only ever get these from Primark because we couldn't seem to find them anywhere else other than Egypt. It was only a few years ago that you could buy sleeves as an accessory. I remember owning a pair in every possible colour in order to wear them with different tops and dresses.

The one thing I found problematic about the scarf is that it always ruined my outfit. That's because there was barely anything available when it came to scarves. We had two options: itchy fabrics with tacky trimmings from Islamic shops, or high-end designer scarves covered in Louis Vuitton or DKNY logos. The latter option didn't have much fabric to play with, so they had to be worn really tightly. Then there was Tie Rack – our one saving grace – but that was about it for a long time, until high street shops finally caught on to scarf mania. Of course, this trend was never marketed towards hijabis but Muslim shoppers finally had more options for headgear.

Of course, hijab is more than just headgear or longer dresses. Many women see hijab as a way of life, focusing more on the spiritual and inner characteristics of modesty rather than just outer appearance.

For some women, outer modesty is the main focus, for others it's a bit of both and for others the inner focus is the priority. All in all, Muslim women are at different levels of faith and are adopting modesty either physically, spiritually or both, at their own different levels each day. It is an independent, personal experience. It can be a struggle, a joy, a journey – each woman has her own unique experience. Ultimately it should always come down to choice and ensuring your emotional wellbeing is thriving.

THREE EASY PEASY EVERYDAY HEADSCARF STYLES

When you're going about your regular day-to-day business, you want styles that are practical, comfortable and inspire confidence. That might mean being stylish, easy or smart – it all depends on you and your needs. Much like a hairstyle, I suppose! And just as with hairstyles, we can get bored with the same look every day. My top tip is to choose scarves made from a fabric that can hold a bit of body but are also easy to drape. My favourite is a blend of cotton and wool. In terms of size, I usually go for a length of approximately 180cm and the width of about 100cm. I always opt for a scarf that is lightweight and breathable, which gives me the option to double the width over when styling. When it comes to colour, if you find it difficult to match your outfit, always go for a nude tone – that complements everything!

So here are my top three easy peasy styles that you can perfect every morning in less than five minutes – even with your eyes half shut!

FIRST STYLE: THE EVERYDAY DRAPE

This look has to be the easiest on the planet. It's literally just the scarf doubled over and draped on your head. I love how simple but super elegant it can look. It's my preferred everyday look, especially during the summer when you're less likely to have outerwear! If, however, you live in the UK and coats are worn most of the year, you can always wrap the rest of the scarf around your neck for a little extra warmth.

SECOND STYLE:
THE EVERYDAY WRAP

This look is for the everyday woman who prefers no faffing around and definitely no fabric flying everywhere. It's neat, stylish and out of your way! But if you want to spice it up for an evening out, all the folds look beautiful when wrapped in a silky material.

THIRD STYLE:
THE EVERYDAY
'MEET ME HALFWAY' LOOK

This style is sort of a mix of the first two. I opt for this look when I need something practical but I also want to keep the style a little feminine. This literally looks gorgeous in almost every fabric. Especially fabric that has a bit of texture to it!

HOW TO BEGIN YOUR LOOK

Before wearing turban styles, I'd always figure out my look by first deciding on what scarf to wear. I used to style it a lot more… extravagantly, shall we say. My scarf was always the most dominating piece of my outfit and it would 'make' my look. Now, however, I like to change my scarf styles regularly, so I would work it around one statement piece, like a nice blazer or a pair of silver shoes. But first, let's go back to the base!

HOW TO CREATE THE PERFECT BASE

I'm a firm believer in perfecting your base in order to get your scarf style to sit just right. If there's one thing missing from online tutorials (including plenty of mine!), it's the steps on how to achieve the shape underneath – which is the foundation of your final hijab look. Choice of fabric plays a big part in deciding how to tie the base, so I'll talk you through three types of scarf fabrics and what styles they work best with.

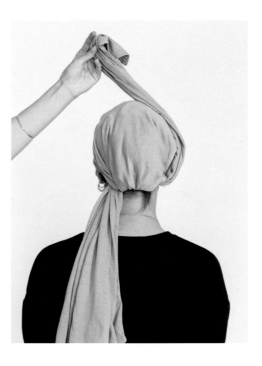

CHIFFON / SILK / MODAL BLEND SCARVES

These sleeker scarves aren't for everyday wear, simply because they're a little more difficult to style, slightly more expensive and work better for special occasions. As the fabric tends to be quite slippery and see-through, use a cotton / jersey headband or a bandana underneath to give it something to hold on to. I always find it best to tie your hair, especially if it's long, into a high half ponytail, just so it sits at the same level as the top of your head. Make sure that you never go higher than your actual head height, though, because that starts to look a little alien-like! Unless that's what you're going for, of course, which I must admit sometimes I do. The half ponytail gives the fabric a bit of width and an even shape. For added 'volume' you can always use a small cotton scarf and wrap it loosely around your half ponytail, creating an even, oval bun shape. If you're like me and have a long face and prefer a little width of fabric around the sides, you can always wrap your small cotton underscarf around your bandana first and then use the rest to go around your half ponytail, keeping everything in proportion with your face as you tie.

COTTON / VISCOSE-BLEND SCARVES

I find myself wearing these scarves on most days, and on the rare occasion of taking part in sporting activities! They're always reasonably priced and can be found in wonderful prints as well as standard plain tones. Most hijabis will have an impressive collection of these. In fact, mine was once on a count of 350 until my wonderful husband decided to take them to the recycling bin during a move last summer, mistaking them for cardboard scraps!

What I find works best for most people is to tie your hair at the back of your head, this time in the middle, either in a regular bun or in a half ponytail if your hair is shorter. If you have REALLY short hair you can always use pins to gather your hair towards the back of your head as much as possible.

It's up to you if you want to use a bandana for extra security. I guess this depends on how long your days are and how vigorous your activities will be! I find that on most days I won't use a bandana as I prefer to have a lighter feeling around my head if I'm out all day. Wrapping around a smaller scarf and a bandana as well as your actual scarf can sometimes be quite suffocating. However, if you go for a lighter feel but worry you're missing some of that volume, you can add some to the base by using one end of the scarf itself. They're always of a decent size, giving plenty of options for adding folds and gathers with the same picce of fabric.

JERSEY SCARVES

Jersey scarves are super stretchy, incredibly comfortable to wear and pretty much suit any occasion. Some of them are quite thin and have smaller dimensions – these are ones I usually avoid. I find the ones with a substantial amount of fabric always look like better quality, plus they give you the option to create numerous looks. Whenever I use a jersey scarf, I tie my hair up into a half ponytail again, but this time at the base of my neck. I then use my small cotton scarf and tie it around my half ponytail, but I make sure it rests on the top rather than around it, as I need to fill in the gap between my ponytail and my head. This allows a smoother 'ramp' to lay your jersey scarf over. Because jersey scarves are stretchy, they're easy to frame the face without getting into the technicalities of creating gathers, folds or forehead points. You can style them without using any pins whatsoever, which goes for both regular styles as well as turban styles.

TURBAN TRENDS

Turbans aren't new, of course; they have certainly been a trend in Egypt for a *very* long time. I was first introduced to a 'Spanish'-style turban when I was about thirteen years old. Many Egyptian girls would add statement flowers, which I found a little tacky and backdated, but my mum, sister and I enjoyed wearing our own versions of this style – sans flower, of course!

When I was older and started blogging, I was reintroduced to different turban looks and traditional African head wraps. I should point out that just before getting back into turbans, I'd started the 'big head' hijab style. Cheryl Cole, singer and former *X Factor* judge, was the cause of that. She always had volumised hair, so my theory was that a volumised headscarf would look just as lovely! It quickly became known as my signature look. But it was Indonesia that gave me the inspiration I needed. When I visited, I met with bloggers out there who wore turbans with style. The Indonesian designer and influencer, Dian Pelangi, was one of the first to rock a turban on the Muslim blogging scene.

But the turban trend was truly kicked off by a Kuwaiti / American blogger and designer called Ascia Al Faraj. Her turban went turbo on Instagram in 2013. She killed it with her edgy, individual twist and that's when there was a sudden boom of girls opting for a turban style everywhere. It's still a hot trend to date.

THREE GO-TO STYLES FOR SPECIAL OCCASIONS

For special occasions, I like to stand out, so I almost always go for a turban-style scarf. If, however, I feel that the outfit could do with some added fabric – almost like it's an accessory – I'll go for a more draped style. My fabric choice is nearly always a delicate chiffon / modal blend scarf. If it's printed, I'll always have it styled into a turban so that the print doesn't overwhelm my outfit choice. Below are my three go-to styles for special occasions.

THE REGAL LOOK

I call it this simply because it's how it makes me feel. I'll alternate between a criss-cross front or a smooth rounded one, usually I'll style my base a lot higher, too, for added drama!

THE ELEGANT LOOK

The look I'll opt for when my outfit
feels like it's missing something. The
drapes create a beautiful flow of fabric
and always look effortlessly glam!

THE CLASSIC LOOK

This is a slightly less dramatic turban
style. Not as high as the first, and one
that will go with any outfit, given the
fabric is a beautiful chiffon / silk mix.
If I feel it's a bit too simple I'll opt
for a more intense colour.

HEADSCARF STYLING FOR DIFFERENT FACE SHAPES

Just as different hairstyles complement various face shapes, so too do scarf styles. After all, scarves are a focal point of your appearance and essentially frame your face. Below are some general tips on how to administer styles that will best complement *your* face shape. Generally, I like to stay away from *categorising* people because life's too short to put everyone in boxes. BUT, the suggestions below will give you a a general idea. However, if you feel you can rock something despite the 'rules', you most likely can! One styling tip that will ensure you pull off anything is having confidence in everything you wear. Walk out of your house like you're the queen bee. If you do that, even a bin bag will look good!

HEART

A wider forehead to chin proportion generally falls under the 'heart' face. This usually means you have some killer cheekbones – cheekbones that deserve to be noticed. Draped styles will look stunning on you, if you keep the front of your scarf at the very top of your forehead and allow the fabric to fall fluidly by the sides of your face. If you're feeling extra fierce one day and want to get those cheekbones up past your eyebrows, bring your scarf down to the middle of your forehead to take away some of its height. Try not to pin your scarf tightly under your chin. Keep it draped a littler lower to elongate it and avoid your face looking like a horizontal rectangle. In my opinion, any turban style is likely to look epic on you, especially if it's draped on one side of your face.

SQUARE

A heavy jaw and square-shaped forehead / hairlines tend to fall under this title. You're likely to have a wonderfully defined jawline and the last thing you want to do is hide it. Having said that, there's no need to accentuate it further, as it needs no help on that score! Feminine folds around the jawline will soften your overall appearance without taking away one of your most enviable features.

LONG RECTANGULAR

If your face is never-ending, with the blessings of a strong jaw *and* a long forehead, you probably fall into this category. I find that creating a fold in your scarf and styling the front into a nice little point works beautifully on you, with the option of pinning it or leaving it to drape under the chin. As for turban styles, try tying the scarf at the top of your head and bringing one side down over the side of your forehead so it just grazes your cheekbone. You can thank me later.

ROUND

If you look in the mirror and the first word that pops into your head is 'chipmunk', this one is for you! The only thing I'd recommend avoiding is pinning the scarf under the chin and wrapping the scarf around your face tightly. You want to avoid a *squeezed* look because, well, that's not a good look for anyone. A flatter edge around your forehead and draping the scarf a lot lower down will add some length to your face and complement the natural curves of your cheeks nicely. Or you could go vice versa and pin it under your chin but leave the scarf to drape loosely around the sides of your face and forehead. I also find that really classic turban styles look super cute on you, so add some more height to your turban look by tying funky knots or a twist at the top!

OVAL

If you find that you have a large forehead, high cheekbones and your face gently tapers down to your chin ever so gradually, it's best to place your chosen scarf on your head and let it do the styling for you. Pin the natural fall of the scarf into place, of course making sure that your base is perfect! You can try lots of different styles, yet the only thing I would say is avoid bringing in the sides of your scarf so it ends up covering half of your eyebrows. In fact, that's a tip that applies to every face shape – NEVER hide the brows!

CHANGING YOUR FACE SHAPE WITH A HEADSCARF

There's beauty in every face shape and the idea with these styles and tips is to help you enhance or complement what's already there. Sometimes, however, we get bored and fancy a change. Maybe you want to accentuate your jaw, make your forehead look shorter, make your face look slimmer, wider, or give yourself even higher cheekbones! Below I've put together some simple steps for each face shape that will help you give the illusion of another face shape.

NARROWING LARGE FOREHEADS

Personally, I love this face shape but I do get a lot of requests from ladies who want to potentially narrow their foreheads and lengthen their faces a little, which just requires one simple step: bring the sides of your scarf a little forward to create an oval shape on your forehead. This will instantly add length to your face and proportion your face evenly.

SOFTENING STRONG JAWS AND SQUARE FOREHEADS

It's common for some women to find this shape somewhat manly – though I think it can be strikingly fierce! I get a lot of requests on how to make a jaw seem smaller or more feminine. By making sure you keep the sides of the scarf well away from your eyebrows, you're automatically adding width to the eye area. This in turn will take the attention away from your significant jaw. Either leave the part under your chin unpinned and let it fall naturally, or if you prefer pinning it for security, gather your scarf along the mid-section of your jaw and underneath rather than starting at the back of your jaw.

SHAPING OUT LONG FACES

Some ladies like to even out their face shape if it seems to be longer than most, especially if they have a long chin and a large forehead. By bringing the top of your scarf down to cover a portion of your forehead, and making sure the width placement between your eyes and your scarf is large, you automatically add more dimension to your appearance, as well defining your cheekbones!

CONTOURING CHUBBY CHEEKS

You might be sick of those chubby cheeks by now if it's constantly making people treat you like a child, but look at the positives – you'll be the one looking like a thirty year-old when you're in fact close to fifty! In the meantime, if you did want to add some contours to your face, all you need to do is let the sides of your scarf drape gently over your cheeks. Using contrasting colours to your skin tone will also help create some shadows in the right places.

MY TOP 10 WARDROBE ESSENTIALS

Over the years I've filled my wardrobe with key and must-have pieces that I feel EVERY woman needs regardless of her style. Whether or not you consider yourself a 'modest dresser', all women have a few things in common when it comes to clothing. We all want comfort, confidence and style, right? Well, below are my top 10 wardrobe essentials that will help you achieve exactly that – with every outfit and any mood that you're in!

YOUR 'GO-TO' JEANS

Denim is such a timeless staple and once you've found a pair of jeans that fit like a glove you'll want to wear them every day, with every look. What's great is, you can! No one can tell if you're wearing the same jeans over and over again. And if they can, who cares? You can go from a casual mum look with a pair of trainers to early evening dinner with some pointy ballerinas.

TRAINERS

It doesn't matter if you've never set foot in a gym or gone for a cold morning jog, you can still wear trainers. Every year or so, I go trainer shopping. I actually wear trainers almost every day and I usually go for a crisp, clean, white pair. I find myself wearing them with almost ANY look. Yes, even skirts. Especially skirts, actually!

> *'I like my money
> right where I can see it:
> hanging in my closet.'*
>
> Carrie Bradshaw

OVERSIZED TOPS

We all have those bloated, lethargic days where the last thing we want to do is worry about fitting into clothes. For me, this is most days! So naturally my ultimate wardrobe staple is oversized tops, jumpers, sweaters, shirts, blouses… oversized ANYTHING, literally. Unless you're super slim, try to avoid wearing baggy bottoms with an oversized top, or break it up with something, like a belt or even heels. The last thing you want to do is make it look obvious that you're trying to hide for the day! Remember, ladies; we're pulling everything off under the 'Style' umbrella, not the 'Bin bag' one!

THE 'SAVIOUR' BLACK TOP

It often happens that five minutes before I need to head out of the door to go to an event, I'm at the bottom of my wardrobe sobbing into a pile of clothes that I just claimed 'I don't have any' of. It's at this point that I ALWAYS go to what I like to call my 'saviour' piece. And it's usually my favourite black top – a boxy fit with a round neck and good structure – mid-length, so it covers my butt, and the front usually a tad shorter than the back (which makes my thighs look a little slimmer). I'll slip this on with a pair of chinos or skinny jeans, fancy shoes, a nice little clutch, oversized coat and a few accessories and I'm good to go!

A CRISP WHITE SHIRT

This piece is so essential to any woman's wardrobe. Just a regular fit, but I prefer one that comes with a bit more length to cover my Muslim butt (again). You can use it for layering, and you'll find that you can't live without it! This piece of standard office attire is going to help you transform every single one of your jumpers, crop tops, T-shirts even!

SCARVES

Oh my goodness, you know those weeks when you feel like every outfit is the same as yesterday's? Oh wait, that's because it literally is. Well, your answer to fooling everyone is a scarf. Change your scarf every day. I don't mean headscarves either, I'm talking about scarves as accessories: around your neck, tied around your wrist, around your bag or even your waist! I love getting small silky square ones with lovely vintage prints and wear them around my neck. Sometimes I'll go for a thicker, larger scarf and drape it over my shoulders as a top. On most days, I'll keep the base simple (black top and black jeans) and then go wild with my scarf around my neck. It makes all the difference.

A GOOD COAT

Sometimes I work my whole look around a super statement coat, but that doesn't mean it needs to be tremendously colourful or busy with prints. It simply needs to stand out and OWN the rest of the look. I'll always go for a 'good coat' outfit when I'm spending most of the day outdoors. I hate it when my clothes bulk up my coat fit, that's why I prefer to keep the coat as the focus, and go really basic underneath!

A BLACK ABAYA

Yep, that long black 'oppressive' garment that some Muslim women wear! But seriously, this traditional dress has been a wardrobe staple for decades. It's the easiest piece to style for WHATEVER occasion, and makes for lovely outfit photos, too, with the right backdrop. Just like with a kimono or a modern-day duster, all you need to do is to wear your abaya open with a pair of jeans, a white T-shirt and sneakers!

BLACK SKINNY JEANS

I know there was a phase when fashion websites and magazines were trying to convince us that skinny jeans were out of trend, but let's face it, a black slimming pair of trousers, usually with a good stretch, is never going to leave any woman's wardrobe. They're comfy, easy and flattering, and are great for those bloated PMT days. I need my black skinnies and no one, neither now, nor in ten years' time, is going to take them from me!

A FITTED BLAZER

A good blazer is so versatile. You can pair it with almost anything and it instantly smartens it – even a tracksuit! A blazer gives off a strong feminine edge. All you really need is one decent black one. Having said that, though, my wardrobe boasts about five different blazers! I have a fitted silver one, an off-white one, a tweed one, and I love my structured blazer with pointy shoulder pads and slim-line sleeves. I'd suggest pairing a black blazer with a stripy T-shirt, boyfriend jeans and a pair of good heels. It's a timeless look.

BAGS

Bags can be annoying and change how an outfit looks on you, but I know that they are sometimes necessary! You can either go bag-free, or if you must wear a bag, I recommend the following options…

BAG-FREE

Yep, I'm starting the bag section with going bag-less! If I'm venturing out for the afternoon without my little one, for a quick meeting or a coffee date, let's say, believe it or not I actually won't use a bag. I like to be as hands-free as possible. Also, sometimes, much like coats, I think bags can be annoying with your outfit. Having a bag on my shoulder changes the way my top looks on me. I know it's such a small thing to notice but I'm all about the details when it comes to my style, so I'd always prefer to go bag-less unless it's absolutely necessary. I'll carry a cardholder that fits nicely into any pocket, and then I'll carry my phone in one hand and my vlogging camera in the other!

TOTES

I find that when I do need to carry something that isn't too bulky, a tote bag will do the trick. Tote bags are fuss-free, they're great to throw random stuff in, and you don't have to think about them too much. If you can pull off a tote bag with your outfit, do it. They look good when they have a slogan or a hashtag, and can complement a casual outfit of jeans, a white shirt and a jumper.

OFFICE BAGS

I love shopper bags, especially the leather ones that keep their shape. Go for black, grey or tan, as white gets dirty – plus they can look super cheap or tacky.

CLUTCH

The only time I'd say a bag either makes an outfit or is a vital part of my look is when I opt for a smaller one or a clutch. But these are more of an accessory, because usually they can only just about fit a lippie in them and nothing else!

MUM BAGS

On a full-on mum day, I need a bag with plenty of space, practicality and style. Unfortunately, most of the bags on the market these days are seriously lacking in the style department. It was frustrating that becoming a mum meant I had to suddenly haul around unsightly brown and blue bags with splashes of orange, and owl or leaf prints! But then I came across smaller, independent designers who are championing trendy nappy bags for parents everywhere. Two of my favourites are Tiba + Marl and Jem + Bea; between them there are options for more casual rucksack-style bags as well as hand-held styles fit for a more sophisticated look!

The great thing about them is they have lots of compartments and hidden places to organise all of your baby stuff neatly. It makes you feel like you have your shit together for once, which helps boost the 'good mum' vibes! There are also loads of other bags not branded as nappy bags that will do the job, if not better sometimes. I used my husband's Jansport rucksack for a good few months. It's all about what you find the easiest and most practical. Never mind what the high street is telling you!

FANNY PACK

You can get some amazing ones these days on the high street. You normally wear them around your waist, but I wear them across the shoulder and chest. They are so easy as they are literally hands-free. I have a tan one and also a glittery one that really helps to bring a drab outfit to life.

FIVE KEY SHOPPING TIPS

Ladies, I know how hard it is to shop for the one thing you went on the hunt for. Too many times I've found myself submerged under a mass of hangers, tangled tags and an aching arm as I stumble over to the till. Only when I get home do I realise the smaller-sized bargains and out-of-season summer shirts are not going to help me get closer to the outfit I actually need for next week's event! But my shopping fails will now be your saviour, as I share my top five tips to get you through an afternoon of shopping shenanigans.

1   Think of your budget and stick to it. The most
     effective way to do this is by taking out cash instead
     of using your card. When the money is physically
     disappearing out of your hands, you're more likely
     to feel the pinch and be disciplined. And if you still
     think you'll resort to plastic once the funds are dry
     – LEAVE YOUR CARDS AT HOME!

2   Pre-plan your trip. Sometimes when I'm off to
     fight with fashion on the high street, I like to make
     a little schedule. Okay, I've never really written it
     down (I'm way too disorganised for that), but
     making a mental note always helps. I'll tell myself
     I've got two hours to go to five shops. If I haven't
     found what I'm looking for, then I'll give myself an
     extra half an hour to have a frantic spree around!
     Some of you reading this might be thinking two
     hours is an awfully long time to browse through
     just five stores. Others might be thinking, 'Girl,
     I can spend two hours just in Zara!' Anyway, I hate
     shopping military style. Shopping is supposed to be
     fun, right? NO. Unless of course you're going for the
     social aspect, but if you need to find stuff, do not get
     distracted. Which leads me on to my next tip.

3   Go alone. The last thing you need is your mum
or sister persuading you to stop for a chai latte and
the whole trip turns into a family therapy session
for hours on the sofa at Caffè Nero. If you brave it
alone, it also means you won't have anyone to hand
shopping bags to when you're getting a bit overloaded,
which means you're less likely to shop for crap that
you don't need!

4   I know I just told you to brave it alone, BUT that
only applies if you know what you're looking for
and know what suits you. If you haven't a clue on
what to get, then obviously scrap the last tip and
take someone who knows their shit, for God's sake!
We're all guilty of making weird fashion decisions
when alone. Prancing about in changing rooms in
front of deceivingly slimming mirrors, we convince
ourselves the bell-bottoms and oversized hoodie
work well together. But now your tag-along
companion will be on hand, ready to slap you back
to reality, tripping you over those bell-bottoms. If
you feel you are clueless, please don't underestimate
the importance of bringing your sister, mother or
friend along.

'Whoever said money can't buy happiness simply didn't know where to go shopping.'

Bo Derek

5   Online shopping. If you're the kind of person who dreads going into town for a wardrobe update, why put yourself through the misery? Just get on the good old internet and shop in those five stores all at the same time. You can pretty much get next-day delivery on almost any online store now, so even if you need something last minute, you're fine! Better yet, there are so many brands that are online only, which is perfect if you're looking for something different. The only downside to online shopping is, of course, that you can't try anything on until it arrives. But honestly, what's better than having a whole pile of new clothes to try on in the comfort of your home? In front of a mirror that will reflect the truth, the whole truth and nothing but the truth! If all fails then have no fear, just send it all back and start again.

KEY LOOKS

*'What you wear
is how you present
yourself to the world,
especially today, when
human contacts are
so quick. Fashion is
instant language.'*

Miuccia Prada

KEY DAYWEAR
LOOKS FOR
SPRING / SUMMER

Living in good old Blighty sometimes means that our relationship with the spring / summer season is somewhat long-distance. However, on the odd occasion we do get a bit of sun peeking out, I like to make sure I'm WELL prepared for it. English weather is unpredictable – it might be the perfect summer's day and then suddenly buckets it down. The weather makes all the difference to your outfit, not necessarily to what styles you might go for, but your fabric choices. I like to have trusty, go-to pieces in my wardrobe all year round.

FIVE SPRING / SUMMER ESSENTIALS

It's a good idea to make sure you have your staples wardrobe ready when the season hits. It can be difficult to transition without a few 'outfit fails', so here are my top five must-haves for spring / summer that will help you get through it without any faff!

A FRESH FLORAL TOP

A gorgeous cotton, linen or lightweight chiffon top is always perfect for summer. The good thing about a floral print is that you don't have to layer it. You could wear a camisole if you want to feel more comfortable, but I find a skin-coloured bra does just the trick!

A TRUSTY LIGHTWEIGHT MAC — PREFERABLY IN A CREAMY CAMEL TONE

Lately I've loved mink shades as an alternative to the standard, though. I find myself turning to a mac on a daily basis, especially during spring. There are so many style variations to the classic now, too, so it's pretty easy to find one that will suit your individual flair and shape.

POINTED BALLERINAS OR PUMPS

They need to be flat, and always pointed, not round. These slim out your legs and look feminine without having to wear a heel. The great thing about them is they look dressy enough to wear out to fancy events. I love them in literally any colour, but for summer it's nice to have a hot pink, bright yellow or electric blue pair.

A GOOD PAIR OF CHINOS

When you find the right ones, they'll be in your
wardrobe for years. Chinos are the perfect comfy
trouser to help you with that season transition.
You can dress them up or down. There are classic
plain colours available every year on the high street;
I like to go for navy or camel ones, but I love it when
I find a pair with a lush print perfect for summer.
Sometimes you can catch them in wonderful silk
fabrics, too. This will completely change up the
classic look, but most importantly still retain the
comfort and coolness that you picked them for!

A HAT OR A READY-MADE TURBAN

A summer hat looks fabulous in the sun and has
a lot of coverage. It's best to wear a lightweight
cotton or viscose square scarf underneath – it
can be printed or plain, as long as your scarf is
complementing rather than competing with your
hat! To change up your headgear, a ready-made
turban is the perfect easy option to throw on,
especially when you're in a rush. You can even
get them on the high street these days!

TWO SPRING / SUMMER GO-TO LOOKS

SMART / WORK

If I've got something a little more formal to go to, I find the perfect combination is a lightweight structured power blazer (usually black or a dark shade; linen blends are always a good choice for this season), a plain white undertop and a pair of slim, tailored cigarette trousers. The colour or print is all yours to decide, depending on individual choice and style! Paired with some comfy pumps or heels, if you prefer, you've got the perfect 'smart but still trendy' balance.

CASUAL / WEEKEND

For this look, I'll go for a long, crisp white shirt, a good pair of boyfriend jeans or chinos, simple black strappy sandals and the scarf of my choice. I normally wear a cotton / viscose fabric and I vary between three styles: turban, turban to the side look with a 'ponytail' fabric coming down, or the classic but draped look. You can jazz up the outfit with a printed bag, a printed scarf or a pair of cute earrings. Also, ring stacking on any outfit can look edgy (I wore 15 rings at one point!). Added to this, I nearly always wear a pair of sunnies – they're a good way to hide half of your face if you're feeling a little insecure with your skin, or if you just don't fancy facing the world that day. Plus, it saves time on make-up!

DAY TO NIGHT

If you've been out all day and have an evening event that requires something a little more 'fancy', fear not! I'll help you 'jzshoosh' up these looks to take them from day to night, without changing the whole look. Think: scarf, accessories, change of shoes and make-up, too.

Take my go-to casual look from the previous page. The only thing needed is to splash on a darker shade of lippy and change up the scarf – either the style or the fabric. If I was wearing breathable cotton during the day, I'd switch to a silky soft scarf to give an instant evening vibe. Alternatively, change what's on your feet. Apparently, most people notice shoes first, so by that theory, if you wear a pair suitable for whatever the occasion, the rest doesn't matter!

As for the smarter / work appropriate look from earlier, try adding some jewellery to capture that evening look. A statement necklace or a bit of bling on a choker will automatically bring the attention to the top half, and if you paint some liner on those lids, your make-up transition is totally transformed. Try tucking in your white top, it will smarten the look instantly. If you choose a small printed silk scarf to accessorise the outfit, as suggested earlier, it'll seem like another outfit completely. Also, if your bag is medium-sized and you can stuff the handles inside and transform it into a clutch, go for it!

KEY DAYWEAR LOOKS FOR AUTUMN / WINTER

When I think of winter, I think of cosy nights cuddled up on the sofa, cradling a mug of hot chocolate and enjoying that fuzzy feeling of warmth. *Sigh*. But then I get real and drag myself out into the cold – but I go well prepared! So let me help you survive this winter in style.

FIVE AUTUMN / WINTER ESSENTIALS

FAUX FUR

Tacky or not, I love it. There's just something about it that gives off a luxurious look that most people can't afford in real life. Whether it's a fluffy scarf, a hooded parka or a full-on cheetah-print jacket, there will always be a bit of fake luxury in *my* wardrobe.

OVERSIZED PLAIN BOYFRIEND SWEATERS

I cannot survive without at least an armful of these. The cold just gets you craving snuggles and big warm hugs. What better way to get a cosy hug out of your clothes, right?

BEANIES

I love beanies as alternatives to scarves, which I sometimes wear to change things up every now and then. They're also a lot easier to wear, yet somehow can still look similar to a turban style. Plus, no one can deny they're suitable for the cold!

KNITTED / RIBBED SKIRTS

Knitwear is an obvious must for the cold weather, but if you ever find a snug-fitting maxi or three-quarter-length skirt that's either ribbed or knitted you will find yourself grabbing it for the office as well as weekend winter activities.

COLLARS

These are one of my favourite accessories all year around, but when it comes to winter they are vital for that extra coverage without the bulk beneath. I've DIYd myself a few because they're not that common on the high street at the moment. But there are endless styles to come up with! These are so perfect to add under any top to make it look like you've layered with a shirt.

TWO AUTUMN / WINTER GO-TO LOOKS

SMART / WORK

For a more refined look, try a snug maxi skirt over some thick black tights, paired with a shorter jumper. It could have a quirky, but not too eccentric print if it's for a professional environment. Layer up with our trusty white shirt that we love so much to perfect that office look!

CASUAL / WEEKEND

You can't beat an oversized boyfriend sweater or a turtle-neck cable-knit combined over some knee-high boots. Classic, comfortable and cosy. Keep your hijab or hairstyle simple for this look and accessorise with some funky glasses and dainty rings for a look that will see you through a long day out or a coffee date with some friends.

DAY TO NIGHT

You're done with your day, but now you need to figure out how to change up your look for the evening – without actually changing. Take a belt you might have lying around, or better yet grab a leather strap off any of your bags and wrap it around your midriff for a bit of waist action with your sweater. If you don't fancy having a bulky sweater on for your evening dinner date, change your jumper to a simple silk blouse or a ruffle dress, keeping those knee-highs on!

If you are meeting friends after work and don't have time to go home, what do you do? Take off that white shirt you used for layering earlier and bring some sparkly shoes in your workbag with you. Swap your footwear in the loos and take that shirt off, add a darker lippy and you're sorted!

MY FASHION ICONS

SHEIKHA MOZAH

If there is one woman who symbolises style and grace, it has to be Her Highness Sheikha Mozah, wife of the former Emir of the State of Qatar. I discovered her when I first started blogging while I was on the hunt to find stylish Muslim women. Sheikha Mozah's look was never girly; it was powerful, structured, yet understated. I think Sheikha Mozah has taught every woman, Muslim or not, that there is elegance and beauty in modesty. She has her own personal style, even the way she wears her turban. She's the only one to pull the look off, but that uniqueness is important – it made me want to find my personal style and perfect that.

DIAN PELANGI

Dian, an Indonesian blogger and designer, was another very different inspiration who also had her own trademark style. She often wore traditional Indonesian fabrics – batik prints that were playful, girly and colourful. They very much reflected who she was, her culture and her environment.

'Fashions fade,
style is eternal.'

Yves Saint Laurent

POP STARS

For a while, looking at celebrities and their show outfits was a huge inspiration for the kind of clothes I was making. I'd change them up to a more modest version, of course. One particular time that sticks out was when I'd first started making clothes and taking part in small local community fashion shows where I was the main stylist. I remember Nicki Minaj was the HOT TOPIC of the day. I secretly loved how she looked and her eccentric style. I would style my models (who were basically my mates helping me out back then) in lime-green scarves as Nicki Minaj's hair was lime green at the time! I dressed them in similar clothes to what she would have worn, but just longer and looser. Back then, power blades (really oversized, massive, pointy shoulder blades) were also on trend, I think it was Rihanna who started it and I loved it. I used to spend ages on the internet finding shoulder pads and I'd sew them together and do photo shoots. By this stage I had bought a bigger sewing machine, a year after my little one. I should point out that I'm over that searching for inspo phase now – I wear what I want, how I want – but seeing these icons certainly helped when I first started blogging.

A NOTE ABOUT FASHION TRENDS

Whilst I don't like how fashion and current trends can take over your life to a point of constant anxiety and obsessiveness, I do appreciate how important they both are in terms of individuality and society. Fashions come and go; even if you're not feeling particularly fashionable in a certain outfit, know that everything you're wearing was totally in at some point in history and it will most definitely be reinvented in the near future. We go full circle with everything in life, and clothing styles are definitely not exempt. The same goes for trends; one minute it's colour blocking and busy prints, the next it's all about minimalism and earthy tones. I actually think it can get very unhealthy to follow fashion trends religiously. You end up being a 'hype-beast' – someone who jumps on the bandwagon but is ready to drop it when the next thing comes out! I do, however, think that trends can help to find your individual style. You know when you've found it when it becomes recognisable amongst your friends, family and peers.

I do enjoy following trends, but usually only if it's something that genuinely gets me excited, or if it's something that works with my look through my own added twist. In terms of fashion and new styles, I feel that nothing is ever actually truly original. Every new design has been inspired by a previous era or culture and reworked. The talent comes in the ability to set the trend by reinventing the original concept with class.

SPECIAL OCCASIONS

Dressing for events can be tricky for everyone, and dressing for special occasions is definitely even trickier for those of us that want to dress modestly. Here are a few of my tricks and recommendations for making every outfit gorgeous!

PROM

Prom can be a difficult time for some of us when it comes to figuring out what the hell to wear. When I had my prom, I'm sure it took up half the year to decide on an outfit – especially on how to wear the hijab with it! Back then, although we were in a very multicultural school, my sister and I were actually the only two girls wearing a hijab at the prom. The rest either took it off or weren't wearing it anyway, so although they still had the difficulty of finding something gorgeous that covered, they didn't have the extra pressure of trying to make a headscarf look half decent with a dress that was clearly not made for modesty! I'm pretty sure prom-goers all across England have made progress with their looks over the last ten years or so since I attended mine. Back then, there really was no help via social media. Even I, lover of all things style, got it completely wrong for prom – I wore a bolero with my dress and it killed the outfit. Plenty of girls email me with their prom dress asking me how to 'halal' it up while avoiding the 'odd combo' vibe. If you want to style something off the high street, do not fear, there are plenty of ways to do it. So, here's what to wear if you're a hijabi / modest dresser and prom is approaching.

WHITE SHIRT SAVIOUR
FOR STRAPLESS DRESSES

Layering a strapless dress with a classic, clean-cut shirt combines two very basic styles. Together, they give a more sophisticated, refined and most importantly timeless look. It doesn't have to be a basic white shirt with a typical collar. There are plenty of different options that will give you a different vibe altogether. A shirt with a high-necked Victorian collar, for example, will give you a regal tone straight away. Who doesn't want to look like a queen for prom?!

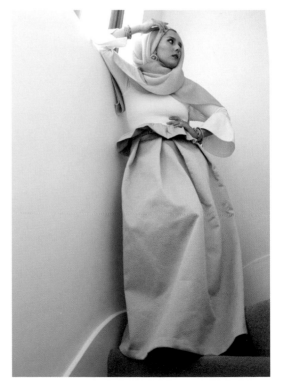

As you might have guessed by now, my favourite staple piece is of course the white shirt! I would wear it with anything – from prom dresses to thick jumpers. Here are my top five places to buy the all-important white shirt:

1   ASOS
2   M&S
3   COS
4   A SUPERMARKET
        (LIKE GEORGE AT ASDA)
5   PRIMARK

THREE WHITE SHIRT LOOKS

And while we are at it, here are three quick and easy white shirt looks.

SMART

Wear a white shirt under a blazer, with the shirt tucked into printed trousers. Top and tail it off with a plain turban and trainers or heels.

WINTER

Wear a white shirt under a short jumper, over a pair of jeans and white trainers, with a plain turban.

SUMMER

Wear an oversized white shirt with chinos and white plimsolls. Accessorise with big hooped earrings and a printed, wacky scarf around the neck.

COTTON UNDERTOPS

When it comes to sleeveless dresses, using cotton tops for arm coverage can actually work quite well, as long as you keep in mind your colour choice and go for something that works, if not totally blends in with your dress. An obvious example is black on black. It's important to think of the pieces you're using for coverage as part of your outfit rather than just something to cover up with. That way you're more likely to look 'put together' than 'nice dress but it's a shame she had to wear that weird top underneath', if you know what I mean.

TRADITIONAL

This is the easiest option. If you're from a culture that has fabulous outfits, like for instance you have Indian saris or Moroccan or Palestinian kaftans, you will certainly stand out amid a sea of high-street blue-, purple- and champagne-coloured strapless prom dresses!

RAMADAN

Ramadan is a time to focus on bettering ourselves, to reflect on our faith and of course to fast for hours on end. This means a lot of self-discipline is involved. For this entire month, I like to dress simply and comfortably – the less complex the look, the less complex my mind is for the day. I find dressing practically and simply can mentally help you get through a long day of fasting, with not as much as a coffee passing your lips! Abayas come out more this month; they're the easiest thing to wear and can look stylish without much effort.

EID

Eid marks the end of Ramadan. It's a time for celebration and fun with family and friends, but most of all it means… eating! And a lot at that. When I was younger, my friends and I would get SO excited for Eid. We'd explain to everyone who didn't celebrate it that it was like our 'our Christmas', just so they'd understand the importance of the holiday. Our parents would give us an allowance to buy Eid clothes and we'd spend ages figuring out what to wear, with endless shopping trips – many of which throughout Ramadan itself actually! All my Pakistani friends bought Asian outfits and looked like they were going to a wedding. But we'd hit the high street looking for new jeans, new heels and new dresses in Zara or H&M. We were never mega dressed up in comparison to our mates, but in recent years, I have been wearing more Arab designs, like kaftans, loose trousers and matching sets, which are slightly more elegant than my high-street purchases! Much like Ramadan, I like to keep things pretty flowy. I'll maybe just add a bit more make-up and a pair of heels to give my look some extra spice!

WEDDINGS

MODESTWEAR
FOR BRIDE AND GUEST

Wedding dress stress is something that every bride has in common no matter where they hail from. Some of us daydream of the big day with no inkling of how taxing it can be to find the 'perfect' dress – especially a modest one. I've seen countless brides having to layer a white lycra, skin-tight top under a strapless sweetheart-cut dress. Warning! This is wedding dress suicide. The same goes for wedding guests in hijab who have to 'halalify' their revealing dresses with whatever mismatching undertops are available to them.

I know I speak for a lot of us when I say we're sick of nothing being available on the high street. Everything is so drab, boring or typical. There's nothing fresh and exciting that actually fulfils all of the requirements – one of them being affordability. It sucks.

Unless you're from a culture that already has traditional modest-friendly bridalwear, it can be nigh on impossible to find ready-to-wear bridal dresses with full coverage. I found my only option was to have my wedding dress custom made.

MY WEDDING OUTFIT

For my wedding day, I decided to go for the traditional ivory bridal shade, and I took my inspiration from a Dior dress that Jennifer Lawrence had worn to the Oscars. I took the photo to the seamstress and asked her to recreate the same dress but with full-length arms and a slightly raised collar. For my headscarf, I was adamant not to do what was expected – a plain tulle or chiffon wrap. At the time, I was obsessed with prints on raw or taffeta silk. So I chose a cherry print taffeta fabric that I wrapped into a turban style, and attached a small bridal veil into a fold. As for shoes, none of that nude or baby pink fabric encrusted with diamantes – I went for hot pink suede court shoes from River Island!

When it came my second dress for the walima, the traditional wedding reception that took place two days later, I searched out bolder fabrics. I wanted a print with some body to it, because I needed my dress to be structured. But it was so hard to find something suitable. Instead I took things into my own hands and ended up going to curtain shops! Curtain fabrics tend to be stronger and hold the shape better, plus they have endless print options.

I found a champagne, floral-print curtain fabric. I absolutely loved it; it was different, daring and beautiful. It was £10 per metre and looked like silk. I got it made by a fashion graduate who had just started her own business. You can find these designers on Instagram these days, which is great!

Curtain dresses hadn't really been done before at weddings, but my dress started a trend. People were inspired and lots of women started considering the curtain fabric departments for their occasionwear dresses. I actually recognised some curtains in a hotel room once, they were exactly the same fabric as my dress!

STYLE OPTIONS

If you don't have the means or time to get a custom-made dress, I've styled some high-street / ready-to-wear options for you. These show what you could wear as a bride or a wedding guest / bridesmaid, be it simple and understated or bold and unique.

VEILS

When we think 'bridal' we often think diamonds, tulle, lace or silk. For hijabis, they tend to incorporate these elements into their hijabs. Often it ends up being a little overboard, because many of us feel we have to make up for not having our hair out. Try to avoid getting too excited. For example, I had my diamond ring on my finger, but if I had put diamantes on my head, it would have taken away from the ring. Be timeless. Less is more.

'To me, clothing is a form of self-expression – there are hints about who you are in what you wear.'

Marc Jacobs

GUESTS

Speaking of overdoing it with scarf bling, it can be embarrassing when guests want to be brides! They stick way too much crap on top of their hijab. When you already have fabric on your head, don't feel the need to overdo it. Think of the fabric as one part of the look already. If you wear traditional outfits, ensure the scarf is simpler, otherwise there's too much going on.

If you're going to a less culturally traditional wedding, I think a jumpsuit is the perfect sort of glam. It's pretty effortless and often has full coverage, and it's easy to accessorise. All you need to 'halalify' it up is wear a little undertop in case the neckline is too low. Or if jumpsuits are not your thing, wear a three-quarter-length dress – smart rather than mega dressy, with cigarette trousers and maybe a silk blazer. And top it off with a neat turban, but don't wear a cotton scarf – raw silk would look best. Details like this are key. Also wear classic court shoes to slim out your legs, and try to match the colour of the heel to your trousers. If you wear black trousers, wear a black heel as it will lengthen your leg. These little tricks of the trade come in handy!

HOLIDAY WEAR

I've travelled so much in recent years, especially since I got married. Generally speaking, every few months I'm on the move! Whether that's for work projects, holidays or even moving to a new house. I have to say I love travelling and exploring new environments. I am lucky to have so many places I can call home. And, of course, with the travel has come the life experience of packing...

There is the obvious thing to consider when you're packing for a holiday: the weather. Holidays often mean plenty of sun, but summer clothes can be transparent, skimpy or short-sleeved. This means that putting together modest holiday outfits for a tropical getaway can be stressful, time-consuming and mean a whole lot of layers. But here are my tips on how to manage your suitcase AND look fabulous on holiday.

'Travellers are the greatest ambassadors of tolerance.'

Queen Rania of Jordan

DINA'S SUITCASE: HOW TO PACK, WHAT TO PACK

ROLL UP

When it comes to packing your suitcase, there's no doubt that being a 'roller' is the only way to maximise your packing space. Especially if you're like me and it's the shoes, scarves, make-up, toiletries and accessories that end up piling way up over your actual clothes. As for tops, scarves and trousers, they all get rolled up as tight as possible and laid into rows. I do try to keep planned outfits together just so that getting ready while away is a little less stressful. Also, ensure you leave some space in your luggage just in case (highly likely) you go shopping and want to bring things back!

MAKE-UP AND TOILETRIES

You thought you could pack those little bits and bobs in all the nooks and crannies at the end, right? Nope. I've learnt the hard way after a bazillion trips and lugging suitcases through to the ends of earth. Packing those bits and bobs first is the only way to do it without completely losing your shit. So, I start off with packing my make-up and toiletries. Obviously the kind of trip you're going on will determine the amount of make-up you end up taking, and the same goes for your shoes and number of accessories.

SHOES

If you're anything like me and rely on shoes and jewellery making your outfit, you've got a problem. Not only are piles of shoes and jewels incredibly heavy in terms of luggage allowance, they take up lots of space. I'd suggest applying the rule of three: take three pairs of shoes with you. First: your everyday pair of comfy trainers; there's nothing crisper than a fresh pair of white trainers on the end of your shabby denims, and don't worry about getting them dirty – just use some 'Crep' spray before you head out. Second: a pair of sandals; aamel, tan or classic white look peach with a neatly lined row of tanned toes, plus they help to give your legs that lengthened look, too! Third: a pair of evening shoes; it's up to you whether it's heels or flat points, but remember feet can get puffier on holiday, so bring your biggest pair!

JEWELLERY

While I used to take way too much, now I simply
take my everyday jewellery – a certain ring and
a bracelet that I never take off. Also, everyone has
their one statement pair of earrings and a bracelet
to take with them. You might also want to pack
a stack of bangles, but I now buy jewellery on
holiday, so I don't feel the need to take shedloads.
Also, I love wearing a nice watch, which can double
up as an accessory.

STATEMENTS AND STAPLES

The best way to make the most of your suitcase wardrobe is to pack key and classic pieces that you can use to create new looks every day.

Loose white shirt: this is a useful suitcase staple. You need a white shirt that's long and loose, yet flattering. Use this as the key piece and then change up your looks with the aid of scarves, shoes and accessories.

Blazer and jeans: take the classic 'repeatable' staples of a blazer and jeans. For daywear, you might pair the jeans with a loud busy shirt and for an evening transition, throw on your plain smart blazer.

Crisp shirt: another staple is a crisp white shirt (you guessed it!) or a light blue pinstripe shirt that gives a slighter smarter edge to the outfit.

Sequined blazer: if you want a statement piece when evening comes, maybe throw on a sequined blazer or loud printed top, keeping the key pieces of the jeans and shirt.

Pleated skirt: throw a pleated skirt in the mix with a plain white T-shirt and you've created numerous looks with just a few items of clothing!

HEADSCARVES

To avoid getting too hot and bothered when it comes to your head, you need to stick to lightweight, breathable cotton. You've got to take into account a whole pile of scarves to match your holiday outfits, including evening looks and outdoorsy scarves for adventurous activities. Try scarves that are neutral and will go with almost any outfit. A lot of browns, beiges and greys, not forgetting a classic black, of course! If you want to add a pop of colour, but still be able to use it for numerous looks, go for a dusted tone. Dusty palettes are beautiful and work well with any complexion in my opinion. Some ladies like to cover up with a hat instead, and why not? When I go away I find I also get braver in terms of trying new styles. It gives me the opportunity to change up my look after my holiday – so I feel like a different woman!

I have a love / hate relationship with the 'burkini', as it's called. I honestly don't understand how and why this phrase even came about. Someone literally took the words burka and bikini, mashed them together and created a word that quite simply has terrified the world in recent years. To the point where some countries wanted to ban it, yes BAN it, for God's sake! Somehow the 'burk' bit of the burkini managed to convince those that oppose it that it's a repressive piece of swimwear for Muslim women. What? Muslim women going swimming are now seen as oppressed? Packing swimwear for a holiday has never been so political! Let's get one thing straight, if anyone takes away a person's choice, then you're the one doing the oppressing. I mean, sort it out!

BURKINI

If you like the burkinis that are available now, go ahead. You've got plenty of patterns and designs to choose from, all in suitable swimming fabric, too. The world's your oyster… which you'll find in the sea… when you're swimming… in your burkini.

DIY BURKINI

Have a look in the cycling section of any sports shop. I like to get a good pair of leggings that you can get in all sorts of super hipster prints now. Then I pair these with a cycling top. They usually come in high necks as well, which is genuinely handy for extra coverage. Then to cover my behind, I opt for a pair of loose-fitted shorts to go over the top, or a sports skirt. This way you're giving yourself the option to mix and match and customise your own 'burkini'. To cover your hair, why not just use a swimming cap? That's if you're actually planning on dunking your head in. I usually just wrap a jersey scarf around my head into a neat, practical and comfortable turban!

NO.4

Beauty

BEAUTY

'Beauty is being the best possible version of yourself, inside and out.'

Audrey Hepburn

MY SKINCARE ROUTINE

I'm very sporadic when it comes to my skincare routine. In fact, you could hardly call it a routine. On most days, I'll roll out of bed, picking up my little one with not so much as a glance in the bathroom mirror. My finger dollops in the first moisturiser it finds on our way to the kitchen for breakfast. I'm spreading margarine on my toast with one hand and cream on my dry skin with the other, only to realise what I've just rubbed into my lips tastes a lot like butter. Glancing down, I find that I've spread Nivea on my toddler's brown toast and she's about to take her first bite. Awkward.

But if you'd like to read about a skincare routine that's more than just dollops of moisturiser or margarine, let me take you through what I do when I have the luxury of time. Having said that, I prefer to keep my skincare routine very simple. I would advise the same to anyone who wants to keep a realistic, healthy and affordable routine.

There are three main ingredients that have worked tremendously for me over recent years.

1ST INGREDIENT: HYDRATION, HYDRATION, HYDRATION

First things first – get a glass, fill it up with water, drink it. Then do it all over again. If you think you've had enough water, you're wrong, have more. I drink glasses and glasses of water and this is probably the most effective part of my skincare routine. It keeps my skin soft, largely spotless and, most of all, feeling young!

2ND INGREDIENT: CLEANSE

I use a cleanser that gently exfoliates and leaves my skin feeling fresh. A personal favourite that's suitable for all skin types is the Mario Badescu Enzyme Cleansing Gel, followed by the facial spray with rose water. I try to avoid foaming cleansers first thing in the morning because they tend to dry out my skin a bit more.

3ʳᴰ INGREDIENT:
MASSAGE AND MOISTURISE

Whenever I've cleansed my face and need to dry it with a towel, the patting technique works wonders compared to hurriedly rubbing it harshly all over your poor face. Always remember: pat, don't rub! I'm also a big fan of 'face exercise' to keep the wrinkles at bay, which is basically a regular and gentle face massage with a moisturiser. My current fave is Kiehl's Hydro-Plumping Re-Texturizing Serum Concentrate or a more affordable one like the Neutrogena Hydro Boost range, which I also love. Both leave my skin feeling soft and almost alert for the day! Also, coconut oil is great for moisturising and I even mix it in with foundations or concealers. Usually if I've opted for oil, it's because I want a very natural, soft and dewy face of make-up. Another current favourite is the Kiehl's Daily Reviving Concentrate. Or I'll sometimes use an SPF that doubles as a moisturiser and sun protection to help keep my wrinkles from getting even deeper! As you've probably guessed, I tend to switch up products! Every six months or so I'll fancy a change – it keeps it interesting and I think it's more likely to be good to my skin.

NIGHTCARE

Equally as important as my magic ingredients is the skincare routine before bed. At the end of the day, I'll grab a face wipe or a baby wipe (recently it's been the latter, as most mums can imagine!) and I'll wipe off my make-up but won't worry too much if it's not all off. Then just before bed I'll go for a facial cleanser, this time one that foams like crazy. Although it's drying, it's the only way my skin feels stripped of ALL the make-up. Then I'll go for that wonderful coconut oil, sometimes almond oil, too, and I'll use a tad more than earlier and massage it into my face, coating it around my eye area and smile lines. It does wonders for wrinkles and over the years I think I've really managed to keep them at bay thanks to these two magic oils! Then I'm ready for bed. And while my skin feels lovely in the morning, my pillowcase certainly doesn't look great. I'm constantly changing them, but to save on washing, you can try placing a soft muslin face cloth over your pillow to protect it. In fact, I should probably start doing that!

TIRED EYES

I never knew my undereye bags could go from 5p bags all the way to Bags for Life in the span of just a week.

A great way to soothe tired eyes is by using an eye massager. I get mine from the Body Shop, but you can buy them anywhere. It's basically a metal ball in the end of a stick, and you roll the gel gently around your eye area. It's so cooling and refreshing. If you want a more traditional and natural solution, use a good old slice of cucumber to get that puffiness down. Although it won't make a massive difference, it definitely helps to soothe and to calm.

JAW AND CHIN ACNE

I always used to tie my scarf ridiculously tight under my chin in fear it would fall off! This resulted in not only an acne problem, but also a huge scab where the pin used to dig in and it would bleed every day. So, my tip would be to LET IT BREATHE. I started wearing my scarf looser, introducing turban and draped styles to give my skin some time to air. But I didn't implement this until I was way older, leaving me with a nasty scar. There's no need to be so militaristic with your hijab style, changing it up regularly is not only healthy physically, it will also help you emotionally in the long run.

Imagine how suffocating it is for your head and neck area to be wrapped up tightly in the same fabric for hours on end? Summer heat is especially problematic, when excess sweat gets trapped in all the nooks and crannies. A lot of ladies in hijab don't realise that washing your headscarves and underscarves is just as important as washing your darn knickers!

If I ever have a bit of extra pamper time I'll pull out a mask every now and then. A really good DIY mask that's helped me with problem skin has been a turmeric-based, yoghurt, honey and lemon mask. I make it fresh at home, and it gives me instant relief and soothes my troubled skin.

DIY FACE MASK RECIPE

2 tsp turmeric
1 tsp plain yoghurt
½ tsp honey
Juice from ½ lemon

Mix the ingredients together and apply all over your face, using your fingers and avoiding the eye area. Keep on for 25–30 minutes or until it hardens. Wash off with warm water and pat dry. Your skin should feel moisturised, but I still add some more moisturiser. If like me you're making the mask for other family members and friends to use, too, use tablespoon measures instead of teaspoons!

BEAUTY BOX BASICS

If you asked me what make-up I can't live without, it would be a good concealer, something for my brows, a bit of bronzer and a balm that can work for both blush and lips. Make-up wipes are a must, and don't forget a good old eyelash curler.

Other than these essentials, below are some non-essential tools that you might like to have in your make-up kit!

BEAUTY BLENDER

Sometimes make-up and make-up brushes can get a little complicated and overwhelming. But thanks to the invention of a beauty blender, that's all you really need. Try it for blending your eyeshadow, smudging out liner, cleaning up messy lip lines and even getting rid of a 'shiny face'.

BLOTTING PAPER

This is something that I've recently incorporated as an essential in my bag, especially if I'm out with a full face of make-up for more than three hours. Blotting paper really helps keep the excess-oil-shine away, and saves you from applying extra powder that might look cakey and clumpy.

CONTOUR BRUSH

I do love a good contour brush, although I could definitely live without one if I absolutely had to. I'm a tad too obsessed with contouring, but I actually tend to stick to the one perfect brush once I've found it. It should be quite large, but narrow in a straight line – a sort of 'gets the job done in one swipe' kind of brush!

ANGLED BRUSH

I don't think I could ever perfect my brows without a precision angled brush. Make sure you get a really small one, as some are too wide. Mine is from MAC, it's neat and has a sharp tip, which is perfect for getting those brows under control! Eyebrow gel also helps, it's like mascara for your brows, and they come in different shades.

TWEEZERS

Many people, at one point or another in their lives, have plucked their brows to oblivion. The basic rule is this: ONLY pluck the extra stray hairs, do not attempt to shape them. If you don't want to tweeze, use a thicker layer of concealer to cover the hairs you want to hide. Or you could bleach them. And don't forget, a pair of tweezers can also do wonders with applying false lashes!

PERFECTING YOUR BASE

Achieving the 'perfect' base is dependent on the look you're trying to achieve and where you're going. When I'm on a regular mum kind of day, I like to do a light coverage look with very minimal steps and layers to the skin. All you need is a tinted moisturiser or a concealer with some bronzer and a little blush to finish the look.

If I'm venturing out for the evening I'll always make a bit of an effort! Brace yourselves – there'll be a few steps to 'perfect' this base! Firstly, I'll use a light moisturiser, especially around my eye area. Then it's straight on to concealer, applying it under my eyes and around any redness using either a beauty blender or a very small concealer brush. Before blending any coverage products into my skin, I will always leave them to sit for at least two minutes. This way you can get even more coverage out of the product, as less is wasted by being wiped away during the blending process. Foundation will come next, a shade darker than the concealer. I lightly dab this in with a beauty blender and gradually blend it up towards the concealer around my eye area.

Then comes the powder, always apply a translucent or light-reflecting powder for the whole face, including under the eyes. In fact, sometimes I will pack the powder on quite heavily under the eyes and leave it to settle there for a few minutes before lightly dusting off any excess. This helps to prevent my concealer creasing and it lasts a whole lot longer. Now I'm ready with a flawless canvas to start sculpting in some cheekbones, and work around the rest of my face!

CONTOURING

I love contouring. I feel like a pancake if I don't contour. (Although I must admit, I do love pancakes too). If you're unaware of what contouring is when it comes to make-up, please allow me to give a little explanation. Contouring is pretty much taking a face and adding some shape and definition to it. If you can't imagine what I could possibly mean, here's my second attempt: if you have a double chin, contouring will get rid of it. If you don't have cheekbones, contouring will give you them. Excited? I was!

You've got two options when it comes to contouring: cream or powder. I save a cream one for special occasions or for when I have the luxury of time. Generally, I'd say a powder contour is easier to apply and control. It also looks a little more natural than cream, but then again who wants natural when you're contouring? Cheekbones to the sky, please!

EYELINER

Gosh, where do I start? There are so many looks you can create with eyeliner – everyday, winged, dramatic. But first, let's make sure the basics are covered, and then your imagination can run wild!

WINGS

This could be an entire page of its own as there are endless wing styles!

To achieve the perfect wing, apply the liner from three-quarters of the way along your eyelid and extend the curve up, as if pointing towards the end of your eyebrow. This forms the upper side of the wing shape. Then bring it back down towards the edge of your eyelid and colour it in. Then apply liner to the rest of your eyelid, but ensure it's thinner as you go towards the inside. Eyeliner is ALWAYS thicker on the outer end. When I'm wearing false lashes, I'll thicken the eyeliner to ensure the eyelash band is covered.

LARGER EYES

To accentuate, add a white liner into your water line to give the illusion of puppy dog eyes. Applying dark liner, or kajal, on to your waterline will do the opposite and make your eyes appear smaller.

BLACK OR BROWN?

Sometimes I prefer to use brown eyeliner rather than black, which seems to be the more popular choice these days. Brown is a lot less harsh, more natural and easier to disguise if you've made a wonky mistake!

GEL OR LIQUID?

I personally always go for liquid, as it's easiest. Find one that isn't too runny. Gel liner is thicker, and not as easy to get right. Plus, sometimes they get really dry. But you can always add a tiny bit of coconut oil to the pot to make it smoother.

EYESHADOW

I only recently became familiar with the world of eyeshadow. In fact, I only bought my first palette a few years ago! There are three basic steps I follow:

Step 1   I'll always go for a soft, reddy brown shade along my crease, all over my lids and blend it like crazy so there are no harsh lines.

Step 2   I'll then take a slightly darker brown and blend that into the outer corner of my lid and then two-thirds along my crease.

Step 3   Finally, I'll use either a shimmered shadow of a champagne colour, or if I'm feeling a little more daring, a much brighter option!

BROWS

I'm sure we're all very much aware of how a good set of brows can 'make' your face. I'm also confident we're all mindful of the maxim, 'Brows are sisters, not twins!' It's very important not to try to make both of your eyebrows exactly the same or to replicate the shape of another person's eyebrows. Have faith that your natural brow shape is custom designed to your own face and really is the best shape for it. Okay, they may need a bit of love and attention, but ultimately, all you need to do is improve what's already there.

EVERYDAY

For everyday use, I'll opt for either a brow powder or even a medium / dark brown eyeshadow to fill them in quite lightly. If I'm not doing a full face, it's best not to do your eyebrows to perfection, as they'll look awkward without everything else to balance them out. If I'm having a non-make-up day, but need to tidy my brows a little, I'll use a brow pencil. I normally use a dark brown one with grey undertones as this matches my brow colour exactly, so that it looks natural with a bare face.

SPECIAL OCCASION

If I'm going to a special occasion and looking for that 'Instagram brow' – a very neat, dramatic and unnatural kind of brow! – I'll apply pomade or a gel brow product with a small angled brush, and fluff up the hairs for volume. The gel dries quite quickly and literally lasts until you decide to wash it off. You can accentuate them even more by using lots of concealer around the eyebrow.

LASHES

I do love me some lashes. Although occasionally I get carried away and end up with them past the tip of my nose. It's amazing how transformative lashes can be to your make-up look. You could spend a good half an hour working on your eyeshadow, but it just won't look complete without your eyelashes curled and brushed through with mascara, or a good set of falsies. There are oodles of different styles available. I really love a set that give the impression that you're wearing eyeliner. If you've mastered the art of applying falsies, not only does this save you time, it's also easier to remove and means less make-up to wash off at the end of the day.

APPLYING FALSIES

This can be very tricky, especially if you're not used to them. But you'll soon get the hang of it. I like to cut my lash strip into three or four sections and apply each section separately. Doing this allows you to control the kind of look and intensity you want, as well as not getting glue all over your lid if you accidentally blink!

SEMI-PERMANENT

If I have a super busy week or I'm going on a trip, I like to get semi-permanent lashes applied at the salon. This means individual lash extensions a process that can take up to an hour. But they last approximately four to six weeks if treated with care. The result is absolutely gorgeous, and means you don't need to use mascara at all! It saves so much time in the mornings. The only downside to getting individual lash extensions is that you have to go back into the salon to get them removed if you decide not to have them longer than two or three weeks. Also, I found myself twiddling and tugging at them, just like I used to do in the past. That awful habit came back to haunt me! But you should definitely avoid this, as you could end up pulling your real lashes out with the fake ones!

The other option is doing it at home. I pick up my favourite pack of cluster lashes and a semi-permanent glue from Ardell. There are different strengths of glue to choose from, but I like to pick one that lasts about two weeks. You can also grab a glue remover from the same brand.

LASH LIFT

If, like me, you keep attempting to curl your eyelashes but watch them sink under a gravitational pull each time, a lash lift is probably the answer for you. Essentially, it perms your real lashes and keeps them curled for up to about six weeks. The treatment is nowhere near as expensive as semi-permanent lashes, and it's a much more comfortable result. It leaves your eyes looking wider, refreshed and highlights how long your lashes actually are. Suddenly mascara application takes no longer than a few seconds and the results are amazing.

HAIRCARE

If you wear a headscarf every single day and have worn it for as long as I have (about eighteen years now), you can understand the toll it can take on your hair. Especially if you're out most days and your head is under all these layers with not much chance for your scalp to breathe. I also find that when it comes to my haircare, it's always left on the shelf compared to everything else to do with 'beauty'. And that's mainly because my hair is always hidden! Having said that, I believe it's so important to maintain healthy hair and scalp. Plus, the last thing you want is to start wearing a headscarf just because you don't like your hair!

Some of you may be surprised to know that a lot of girls wearing scarves actually have some really whacky hairstyles underneath! I know girls who have platinum-blonde pixie cuts, mermaid ombre hair and amazing perms. Some even have the sides of their head shaved! All in the name of fashion and beauty, of course. Just as with make-up, most women do their hair for themselves because they get to see it every day and feel fabulous and confident with their individual looks. Also, a lot of us are married and like to show off different, fun hairstyles to our doting husbands, not to mention displaying our lovely locks at girly afternoons with our friends and family!

UNDERSCARVES

I think underscarves play a big part in allowing our heads to breathe. I like to use soft breathable cotton bandanas to keep my hair back, but never too tightly. Having your hair up tightly all day under non-breathable fabrics is just going to pull out hair and suffocate your scalp. It's also important to keep underscarves clean, so make sure you bung them in the wash regularly!

COCONUT OR CASTOR OIL

Similar to my skincare routine, coconut oil is something I rely on heavily for my hair. Every fortnight or so, I'll douse my hair in coconut or castor oil and wrap it up in a towel for the night, washing it out in the morning. It's really helped to keep my hair thick and soft while wearing the hijab. Massaging the scalp is also great to stimulate follicles for better hair growth. Hair tablets are also a must, I buy mine from Holland & Barrett.

DAYTIME GLAM

Sometimes, or maybe quite often, you want to look glam, even in the daytime! This is my go-to daytime glam look – the perfect look for when you've got something going on that isn't just work or a supermarket shop!

FACE

Apply your base. I use a concealer in my foundation shade and apply it on all of those problem areas: under my eyes to cover dark circles, the sides of my nostrils, over blemishes here and there and just under my brow bone.

I then very lightly dust a translucent powder for my face and under my eyes to set the concealer. It's important to keep it light so as not to get it too cakey, especially in the sunlight!

For contouring, I use a contour stick just below my cheekbone and pull lightly down towards the corner of my mouth, but not quite reaching it. I also apply it to the ball of my chin and across my jaw line, the tip of my nose and finally across the top and sides of my forehead.

Now to highlight those cheekbones! Apply a warmer highlight if your skin tone is similar to mine. Try to follow that natural 'C'-shape curve under your eye socket and towards the apple of your cheek.

Finally, blush. Here I opt for a rose-brown shade and apply it on the apple of my cheeks and also drag it upwards slightly along my cheekbones to keep my cheeks lifted even without smiling.

Let's start with the eyebrows. I like to use a powder for the daytime, as it tends to look less painted on than a gel. Never opt for a black filler if your eyebrows are naturally a dark brown and sparse like mine. Opt for a dark brown powder for the last two-thirds of your brow and a medium brown for the first third, as this will give your brow a natural gradient.

Use a concealer on top of your brow and on the brow bone to neaten and clean up any mishaps that are bound to happen. Then you can apply the same highlighter used on your cheekbones, but this time on your brow bone.

Now for your eyeshadow. I've kept this quite subtle, with the aim of brightening the eyes. Apply a taupe shade into your crease and up towards your brow bone.

I then choose a cream / white shade and pat it all over my eyelid as well as the inner corner of my eyes.

Now comes the eyeliner. This can be difficult if you're not used to wearing it every day. The key is to take your time and if you make a mistake, DON'T PANIC! You won't need to start the eye all over again, just grab a damp cotton swab and carefully wipe away any mistakes. One of my musts for the glam look is having a winged liner, but I only apply it to the outer half of my eye and not all the way across my lid. That way it leaves us something to add when we need to transition into an evening look. Start by drawing a line from the outer edge of your lid at an upward angle towards the end of your brow. Just use this as direction, not a destination! Carry on that line down towards the middle of your lid, then colour it in.

Lastly, lashes. If you're lucky and have naturally luscious ones, you're good with mascara! If you're like me and you have lashes that are straight, point downwards and refuse to cooperate with curlers, go for a wispy pair of fluttery lashes to complete the look.

LIPS

Line your lips with a light brown
/ nude shade. Fill in the outer corners
of your lips gradually until you get to
the middle of your lips.

Then grab your chosen lipstick shade.
I normally go for a rose-brown matte
liquid lipstick. Start your application
from the middle, working towards
the edges. If you do use a matte liquid
lipstick, make sure you moisturise and
exfoliate them beforehand as they can
be terribly drying.

NIGHT TRANSITION MAKE-UP

I find when I have so much going on in the day, I always end up making a few changes to what's already on my face. This not only freshens it up, it also transforms it altogether. There are three super simple steps that I do to change this daytime look to night-time glam.

Step 1   I add eyeliner along the rest of my lid all the way to the outer corner of my eyes.

Step 2   I grab a black kohl pen and apply it to my water line for instant drama.

Step 3   I simply change my lippie to a darker, more prominent and glossier shade.

Parenting & Family

HERE COMES THE BABY

"'I think we've got this parenting gig NAILED,"" said no parent ever.'

Anon

The idea of pushing a little human out of me was the biggest fear in my life, but I also thought that looking after this little human would be a breeze.

Yeah, try NO, Dina.

Labour is one of the most difficult things you will ever endure, but those first few weeks of your baby's life are a million and one times more difficult than anything you'll ever imagine. Well, it was for me anyway.

I spent zero time thinking about what life AFTER birth would be like and spent all my time reading up on labour tips. I also focused on looking half decent, and concentrated on exercise to ensure I didn't put on too much baby weight. Another thing that consumed my time was figuring out whether or not I'd be getting an epidural for the delivery!

Without doubt, giving birth is mentally and physically overwhelming, whether it's by C-section or vaginal. I've heard way too many people say, 'Women have gone through this for thousands of years'. NOT helpful. Mothers need more support and more empathy and don't need to be patronised. But more than anything else, we need to know how to cope when the baby is here.

Looking back, I wish someone had told me to start preparing myself as to how to take care of a newborn. Like changing a nappy. Yep, I didn't know how to change a nappy! The first time I had to do it, I almost freaked out. This might sound kind of pathetic, but let's face it, there's no real preparation for parents, we're expected to *just get on with it*.

Although I don't feel like I actually experienced postnatal depression, which is a very serious condition, I feel like I was very close to it. It's difficult to try to explain it, but having a baby was such a shock to the system. My system, Sid's system, even the cat's system! I found myself

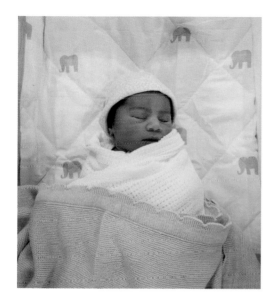

bursting into tears for what seemed like no reason. This happened every couple of hours or so, mainly while breastfeeding. I'd look down at my daughter and have the realisation that I was responsible for this little human. She seemed so tiny and fragile, how would I ever know how to take care of her? Sometimes I'd cry just because Sid would ask me how I was feeling. And of course I'd cry without fail every time the baby cried. Even when she smiled in her sleep, I cried!

For some mothers, those precious newborn days can be bliss, but for others it can be a very dark place. I found myself in a whole other world when our baby Hana arrived. I lost track of time. My days rolled into one. I was in tears every five minutes over I still don't know what. I felt alone, trapped, scared and had an overwhelming sense of responsibility. No one around me really understood what I was going through. I didn't really get it myself. The idea of talking to someone about what I was feeling petrified me. People would think I was a bad mum and they'd take Hana away from me. They'd think I didn't love her. They'd notice that I can't even change a nappy properly, that I wasn't confident holding my baby, that I couldn't even take her for a walk alone. My paranoia was pretty bad and overwhelming!

I don't know what I was feeling; I just know I wasn't happy or sad. Maybe that's just what shock feels like, a huge surge of overwhelming... ness? It got to a point where Sid was questioning why I wasn't happy when we'd just had our first baby. I'd reassure him that I was happy, but the truth is I didn't know what was happening to me. The first ten days were the most difficult. Even though I had my family over for a few days, and I had Sid, it was the loneliest I've ever felt. I tried as best I could to suppress my feelings and be 'strong', worried I'd be judged as incapable, or over-possessive, or crazy even, but it was so difficult to hold it in. I ended up having terrible mood swings. I soon began to appreciate my mother, and all other mothers for that matter! I can't even begin to imagine how any single mothers are able to cope. You women truly are the definition of heroes!

Being called a mum still sounds so alien to me. After I gave birth and brought my baby home, it felt like I'd been run over by a truck fifty times. I was completely and utterly exhausted and had no time to recover, because now I was a MUM.

And, of course, there are those inevitable changes your body goes through. Although my stomach went down pretty quickly, and my weight got back to normal, my body still isn't the same. You feel wobbly and your chest area is now as big as your great-granny's was at the best of times. Sometimes I get this weird feeling even now – a feeling of disgust. Disgust at my body. I was disgusted at the sight of boobs all day, every day when breastfeeding. And then I get disgusted at random things like the fact I'd been sitting in the same spot for hours, nursing and changing. It's a very strange mood to be in.

You suddenly go from being fully free (you don't realise until then how much freedom you had in your previous life) to having this little human as your ultimate priority. Everything, and I mean EVERYTHING, you do revolves around the baby. When to pee, when to brush your teeth, when to eat, when to get dressed, shower, talk to your friends, wash your hands, moisturise your face and, most importantly, when you will sleep... Aaah, sleep, how you are the stranger to me now.

It seems impossible that you will ever be able to establish a routine, and retain your sanity, never mind trying to get back into work or getting back into shape. I can't even take the baby out without it feeling like a mammoth task. I even hate taking her anywhere that requires a car journey by myself.

THE IMPORTANCE OF A SUPPORT NETWORK

I'm a lot better now, thank God. I realised what I needed was my family around me, Mum especially. Sid's support is so vital, but sometimes a girl just needs her mum. So I went and stayed in Cardiff for about ten days and it was almost like a crash course in motherhood.

I think it's fundamental to have a support network around you, both physically but also, more importantly, emotionally. If it's just you and your partner, it's important to communicate your feelings and it's so important for your partner to be aware of the baby blues, even if they don't 'get it'. They just need to be there and listen when you need to sob your heart out over 'nothing' and for when you get those crazy overwhelming realisations. They also need to understand that what this new mother is going through is far from silly. She is not complaining. Don't underestimate how dangerous it can be to let her continue in sadness; it's so easy to become trapped and end up in a downward spiral into this strange, unknown unexplainable darkness.

BUT, it does get better. When you really focus on the positive rather than the shocking changes you're facing; when you start becoming a nappy changing pro; when you become a burping pro; when you get a small rewarding smile from your little human; when you somehow manage four hours of uninterrupted sleep; when you figure out a comfortable nursing position; when you manage to brush your teeth more than once that day; when your partner tells you you're superwoman; when you start having fun dressing up your little human; when you cuddle your little human; and when you get random bursting feelings of pure love for your little human… that's when you start to enjoy motherhood. More importantly, you enjoy your little one.

Children are such a huge, huge blessing from God and they really do bring a whole new meaning to the purpose of your life. So when you do manage to escape those post baby blues, you will never be able to imagine life without them.

Nothing will ever prepare you for a baby, it is normal to feel like that and it's important to talk about it. We need to be babied, we need the support. I managed to fall out of my dark episode. It helped when I moved to London when Hana was five months old, as it meant I then had support from my mum and sister. But I still find it hard. New mothers need someone who's been through it who completely understands how you're feeling. My mum totally understood me. You can have the most supportive husband in the world, but they'll never fully get why you are depressed – which is fine, as long as they don't judge you for it.

Slowly, as Hana got bigger, things started to get better. I ventured out more; still not alone but at least I got out. The days would be so much better when some of it was spent outdoors. I started to enjoy motherhood and cherish every moment of little Hana's growth and now it truly is a wonderful experience that I wish every woman who wants to can one day feel.

'Lucky is the woman whose first child is a daughter.'

Prophet Muhammad
(peace and blessings be upon him)

WORKING
WITH A BABY

Having a baby really kicked me into gear in the best way. When I found out I was pregnant, I went into panic mode, giving myself nine months to work harder than ever before, so that I could take some time off when Hana arrived. Of course, I still blogged when she arrived. I mean, come on, I had to document motherhood somehow. If not for me, then at least for Hana to see when she's older. After getting used to having a newborn around, Sid and I suddenly became super organised.

When I think back to pre-baby days, I cringe at the thought of all those unproductive hours that just flew by. That's just life, I suppose, a part of growing up, too. I never thought I'd see the day where my thoughts and actions would remind me of my own mum!

I'm lucky that I can work from home and not worry about going back into work when maternity leave is up. I really feel for you mamas out there who don't get that choice. If I could barely leave my child when going to the bathroom, I can only imagine how difficult it would be to leave her while going to work, let alone with a stranger. I feel for all the mamas out there struggling to make ends meet, and for all the single mamas – I really don't know how you do it. I can barely do it with a husband who's equally as involved in parenting as me. Nowhere in the world is being a mum appreciated or praised enough, nowhere near as much as when a woman is working. Let me tell you, being a stay-at-home mum or dad is the hardest, most intense and selfless job on this planet. There are no days off, ever. You're working forever and every mum, whether stay-at-home or in an office, is a working mum.

BREASTFEEDING

Once upon a time, I owned a pair of boobs that didn't touch my toes without a bra. It was a time when I could get away with wearing almost ANY style top. It was back in those days that I had no idea of the struggles that my 'heavy chested' girlfriends went through when they'd complain that they weren't able to wear loose tops without looking like tents. But I can safely say that I've now experienced it all: the perky, the sag and the bouncy. Now, I'm probably somewhere in between the three... with one year of exclusive breastfeeding to thank for it.

I'd made the decision to exclusively breastfeed with no help from any bottles before giving birth. Three months in, I was hating my life. I had absolutely zero time to myself, because I was the only source of food for my child. Of course, we tried pumping and offering milk in a bottle, but Hana being just like her mama, a sassy diva, was having none of it. She absolutely refused any teats other than the real thing for just over the first year.

There's no denying that breastfeeding is nothing short of a miracle. I mean, just imagine, you're literally feeding and nourishing your own child from your boobs. Boobs that are right by your heart. Food and love. How wonderful is that when you really think about it? And when I do, I get broody again. It's madness how broodiness overcomes us randomly. I guess it's nature doing its job. As women would never choose to go through the whirlwind of physical and emotional stress that having a baby brings all over again!

For something that's so wonderfully natural, it's also bloody painful. Especially those infamous first six weeks that everyone says are the hardest. Well, I hate to break it to you, but it doesn't get easier after that either. In fact, it gets harder if anything. I never quite got used to breastfeeding, despite the fact my little one was on it ALL the time. I literally felt like a cow being milked, and that I was good for nothing else. It seemed I couldn't stop her crying without my boobs. I couldn't put her to sleep without them. Even when she was perfectly happy not crying or sleeping, she was just suckling on the end of one of my, by now, very sore nipples. I was a milk machine.

I feel that, for me, breastfeeding may have caused my spiral into post-natal depression, even though at the time I couldn't understand, explain or pinpoint it myself, never mind anyone else. It's such a common thing, but it's shocking how little education there is on the topic. It's your mental health at the end of the day, and just as we regularly go to the dentist and doctor for check-ups, shouldn't we be doing the same for our minds?

The subject of mental health is taboo amongst society as a whole – take a look into the Muslim community and it's even more of a testing topic. For some unfortunate reason, mental health amongst Muslims is never taken seriously. If you fall into depression or suffer from anxiety, let alone more complex mental health conditions, the attitude is that you're not 'religious enough'. Or you are scaremongered into thinking you're being possessed. This is an attitude of fear, ignorance and denial, which has to be challenged.

MATERNITY WEAR

Let me get this off my chest – maternity wear is flipping awful. There's literally nothing out there catering for the modern-day stylish mama. It's like they have a maternity wear rule book that says: 'MUST MAKE EVERY PIECE STRIPY WITH POCKETS.' During my pregnancy, I don't think I bought even one piece of maternity wear, other than nursing bras! (Even they are awful.)

During my first trimester, I panicked, thinking my stomach would grow huge overnight and nothing would fit! In reality, I didn't even have a bump showing until I was past the six-month mark. Seeing as the majority of my wardrobe is pretty oversized anyway, I really didn't have any problems with clothing until the very last few weeks when I was practically waddling everywhere. And by that time I didn't care what I was wearing anyway!

TROUSERS

When your bump finally grows and you're a high-waister, you'll probably need to invest in a good pair of maternity jeans. If you're a low-waister, you'll just carry on wearing your trousers under your bump. They should still fit for the majority of your pregnancy unless you're suffering from added bloating and swelling everywhere, of course, or if your cravings have taken over and they just so happen to be red velvet cake, plain bread rolls and cheesy pasta... ahem.

I did come across one particular accessory that was actually a lifesaver for me during and post pregnancy. Let me introduce you to the Love Your Bump waist expander, which does pretty much that! It gives you different sizing options, which is super handy while your bump grows, as well as different fastening options so you can pretty much wear it on all of your trousers and skirts.

BREASTFEEDING TOPS

When you're breastfeeding it's always a juggling act of feeding your baby and keeping your assets covered at the same time! I know there's a breastfeeding cover (basically an apron) that you can use, but when your baby starts flailing his or her arms about, it's not so genius any more. Tops with splits or slits on the side are fab for breastfeeding and pregnancy bump growth in general, too, unlike button-down shirts that I found impractical. I prefer to find tops that allow me to get my boobs out with as much ease as possible while out and about. Let's face it, it's never easy to get them out in front of strangers who look over awkwardly at breastfeeding mamas as if we're making *them* uncomfortable. I mean, how are cleavages socially acceptable, but not women actually *using* our boobs to nurture?! Ugh.

DIY TOPS

Nothing is ever going to make you one hundred per cent comfortable, but at least we can try to help ease the faff just a little. All of my oversized tops really weren't suitable because the collars were quite high. Also, I didn't fancy sticking my baby fully under them because she never seemed to settle like that. As a newbie breastfeeder, I really needed to see what I was doing in order to get her to latch on properly. So my DIY breastfeeding tops consisted of tight cotton undertops into which I'd cut massive holes around the boob section. This allowed me to lift up my overtop and not worry about my stomach being on show while still having coverage around the breast area. This also saved me from having to carry extra scarves in my already bursting bag.

TEAM EFFORT

As a mum who does have to work, I'm so thankful
to have Sid by my side. We're able to split parenting
and household responsibilities equally. Honestly,
without Sid I genuinely would not have been able
to accomplish even half of what I've done so far.
He loves being a dad just as much as I love being a
mother and gets really stuck in. Okay, we do things
differently and argue about the way they should be
done, but ultimately, he's not what some might say
a 'typical dad' – only helping out when it suits.
I actually think a hell of a lot of men should take
a leaf out of his book and get rid of the 'manly ego'
that prevents them from changing a damn nappy
every once in a while!

It can get difficult and stressful for both of you
to juggle your lives with the baby AND keep up with
both sides of your families. It can cause unnecessary
rivalry about who gets to spend time with the
grandkids. So I'm going to leave you with a few
points to consider in my attempt to help you attain
a healthy, balanced work / social / personal life.

PUT YOURSELF FIRST

And by that I don't mean make sure you're sorted
for dinner and then stuff everyone else. I mean
emotionally. If you're feeling like things are getting
on top of you (like the laundry) and you're about to
explode, take some time out for yourself. Everything
else can come later. The dishes in the sink, changing
the bed sheets and the supermarket shop can all be
done later. I like to book myself in for an hour at the
salon for a pedicure, anything to get my mind off
things and just zone out for a bit. I'm sure your
partner won't mind taking over if you've bargained
that he can have his hour later on the PS4!

GO OUTSIDE

Here's a scenario: you've all woken up around 5am on a Sunday, toddler is running around the house like crazy, and you and your partner feel like you're going bonkers. Go out. Out as a family. Even if it's just a stroll around the block. Don't let the rain be an excuse either, it's magic what fresh air and puddles can do for kids, as well as adults. Well, not so much the puddles for us but the fresh air, yes!

SWITCH OFF THE TV

When Hana was tiny, I vowed she would never watch TV and we'd be the kind of family burrowed into books and building things all the time. Who was I kidding, my telly's a bloody saviour at times! But having said that, don't rely on it, and don't let it take over as background noise – it's easy to leave it on without even realising. Sometimes I wonder why I'm feeling so jumpy and unsettled, and then I switch the TV off and it's so quiet I can suddenly hear myself think. Sid and I can unexpectedly have a conversation and Hana is suddenly not irritable either. My stress levels have instantly decreased!

STAY ACTIVE

For example, it was a late Sunday afternoon and I was feeling lethargic all day. After two cups of coffees failed me, I decided to put some music on and have a boogie around my living room floor. I ended up having crazy fun and bonding time with my toddler. I burned off the 'scones for breakfast' calories, managed to get my energy levels back up AND she was knocked out for her second nap of the day! Two birds with one stone? Try four, mate!

RAISING YOUR CHILD

Being raised as a Muslim myself, it's only natural I would want to raise my child as one too. It's also natural that I'd want Hana's upbringing to be nigh on identical to how I was raised. Well, almost. The older I get the more I question some things, or the way I was taught – not just by my parents but also by the people around me. I had a wonderful childhood filled with nothing but memories of love, innocence and fun. I didn't grow up too fast and my parents encouraged us to live our childhood to the max. But that doesn't mean I shouldn't reflect on certain things and wonder if I would do the same with my little one. When I look at the outcome of my upbringing, it's hard to decide whether or not to do things a bit differently, because overall my parents did a great job. They now have four fairly decent human beings as a result!

But I can't help but feel I may need to tweak some things here and there when it comes to small aspects of my child's life. Because, let's face it, society has changed since I was a little girl. I like to think our family has core values that will always be instilled, but I also believe we need to work with and adapt to the surroundings as our generations grow.

Consider cultural teachings or traditions. If we were to step outside of the cultural box to see a different perspective, we would see how bizarre or sometimes how damaging some traditions can be. I'm especially thinking about some restrictive Egyptian traditions or cultural expectations. I hope I would never enforce those ideas on my children. It's easier for some people to let go of than others, though. I guess it depends on how strongly some customs are followed. The question I constantly get asked is if I will make Hana wear a headscarf or 'hijab'. My answer's always the same, that I would like her to be able to come to her own decision about

whether or not she really wants to cover her head.
I would support her either way, but I hope that I am
able to teach her the meaning of modesty as a whole
and offer her a broad and open-minded understanding
of it. I want her to come to her own conclusion, to
nurture her own interpretation of respecting herself,
dependent on her context and her own realities.

SID'S TAKE

Sometimes Sid and I clash on our parenting
decisions. It's funny because when we got married
I didn't even consider what his views were on
raising a child. But I'd suggest to any of you looking
for a spouse, find someone on the same wavelength
as you in terms of what you want for your children.
All the arguments and small differences Sid and
I have now on raising children could have been
easily cleared up in the early days!

Of course, it's a learning curve. I could sit here
and talk all day about parenting and how I think it
should happen, but the reality is I'm just a beginner.
I never stop learning, or making mistakes. There's
no right way to parent. Even though Sid and I clash
at times, I fully respect his choices… ish! Anyway,
it's only right to give you some of Sid's thoughts on
parenting seeing as it is teamwork for us and we very
much split our choices and duties right down the
middle, 50 / 50!

Incoming, Sid's little section of his thoughts
on parenting. Warning, take the following with a
pinch of salt...

SID

'I am a dad, furthermore Hana's dad. I wonder if my dad went through the same fatherly experiences as I have? If so, why didn't he stop at one kid? He couldn't have done jack shit! I'll be honest, being a dad is hard work. You are responsible for this little thing that eats, screams and pushes vibrant smelly parcels out of her bum. Which sometimes (most of the time) I have to clean up! These smelly parcels are wrapped up tightly inside other parcels (nappies) and most of the time thrown over the side of our bed for us to step on every morning… nice.

But other than that, life is great. I was asked (ordered) by the author of this book to give my two cents on how I would raise Hana in the years to come, and honestly, I have no fricking clue. I'm a "take it as it comes" kind of guy. You can't ask me, "Sid, what are you going to do when Hana starts liking boys?" and expect me to come up with an honest answer. Because I think no parent ever really knows how they're going to handle a situation until it happens. Well, that's the same for most things in life. For example, I didn't know it would take a whole forty minutes to drop Hana at nursery this morning, because I hadn't planned the night before! I mean, who the hell plans traffic anyway? Talking about cars, ours is a pigsty inside. Hana ate cake in her car seat the other day, and when I say "ate" I really mean, she smushed it in her hands and threw it all over the floor, but not before wiping it all over the seat and my headrest. How she managed to reach it, I will never know. But I can't bring myself to wipe her little paw prints off because they're cute. When I get to the moments where I'm like "did this little shit really just do that?", I put myself in her shoes and her little T-rex-proportioned body, and I realise she can't do anything without us. And that her pea brain is working twice as hard to comprehend the things that we find the simplest. So yeah, Hana, one day you'll grow up and think you're smarter than us, and you know what? You probably will be, much like how we feel with our parents now. But just know this... I taught you everything you know.'

So, there you have it, you've heard a snippet from both sides of parenting. There's much more we could both say, but if it's not spewing out now, it's probably because we're yet to experience more. Which leaves me wondering, are we ever going to be able to manage life with baby no. 2?

Dina's Reflections

MIND, BODY AND SOUL

'I myself have never been able to find out precisely what feminism is: I only know that people call me a feminist whenever I express sentiments that differentiate me from a doormat.'

Rebecca West

LOSING IT

Brace yourselves, a rant is coming.

I, like most mums I guess, find myself struggling in the constant chase for the perfect work / life balance. What is the ideal anyway? Is it when you've managed to keep stress at bay? Got yourself a decent social life? When you can keep up with the housework and deal with 'mum guilt' if you've spent ten minutes browsing your Instagram timeline? Never mind being a good wife to your poor neglected husband! I think it would be nigh on impossible to find a woman who can honestly say they've figured it all out without secretly losing all sense of themselves and throwing their sanity out of the window!

When exhaustion makes me forget what day it is, and my memory has decided to swap itself with that of a goldfish, and the pile of washing is towering over my head… all I really want is to sit on the sofa (amidst dirty nappies) and catch up on a whole week of *EastEnders*. It's no wonder I feel like a failure on most days. And then there's my 'emotional well-being' to consider, too. I mean really, there are only two options: a) focus entirely on your inner contentment and leave the house looking like a pigsty, or b) manage to get on top of all the housework, while being shattered, going mental and hating everyone who mutters as much as a mere whimper around you.

Try explaining any of the above to your partner, as they constantly wish you'd tell them more, and then the minute you do, you have a hysterical half hour because you've bottled it all up for so long. They then look at you like you've lost your marbles and think you're ungrateful because, actually, they've been washing their one measly effing plate after themselves three times this week! THANKS A BUNCH, HUBBY – that one clean plate has made all the difference!

Deep breath, Dina.

Rant over, thanks for hearing me out.

KEEPING SANE

Now, here's what I actually do when things have gone out of my control and I want to bring some stability back into my life.

I demand a break!

Be it for a few hours or for a few days, dependent on stress levels, of course, but I NEED my time off. Don't ever make the mistake of *asking* for time off, ladies, *inform* whoever is taking the reins from you that you are doing so and so for this amount of time. And then proceed to do it. It might be spending the evening over at your sister's, going out for a coffee with a friend, or taking a long drive blasting your favourite music all by yourself. You will see the wonders of 'me time' unfold, even if it's simply having a hot bath, undisturbed. I think it's so important to enjoy your own company and give yourself time to reflect on your day. Not only are you relaxing your body and giving it some much-needed rest, you're also keeping your mind in check. Having your thoughts to yourself for just ten precious minutes is a must for keeping sane.

THE G FACTOR

Seeing as I am a Muslim, I think it's important to mention prayer. To be honest, it applies to any woman of any faith when I say how important prayer is to your spiritual well-being. Whether you consider yourself practising or not, whether you pray consistently or erratically – ultimately prayer is a time to reflect and connect with a higher power. When I was growing up, prayer was made to seem more of a chore, rather than precious one-on-one time with your creator. The older I've become, the more I begin to view things within religion differently, prayer being one of them.

In all honesty, I can struggle to keep up with my prayers, but when I do, I see it as a time to unwind, reflect and directly connect with God. This means you're much more likely to be consistent and enjoy your prayers rather than seeing them as a burden. Sometimes I literally use the time after my prayer to speak to God – in the most casual manner! I talk about things on my mind, my worries for the future, and I thank God for all the good in my life. When I pray like this, I find it's almost therapeutic and I feel a hundred times better than I did earlier.

If you're not religious, there is always mindfulness. It's so important for all of us to take time out and be in tune with ourselves. The world goes by so fast and the days roll into one and can seem like a blur. So it's important to have the time to focus, breathe and find a bit of peace in all the chaos. It will seriously do you wonders.

BOTTLING IT UP

I'm the kind of person who deals with stress by lashing out at those closest to me. It's not ideal! The thing is, I keep it all in, and let it out in snaps every so often, whilst chugging on with life. Until one day I'll explode and all hell will break loose. Then I feel guilt. I'll sit there sobbing, wishing I'd opened up earlier, but of course it's never that simple, is it?

I've noticed since becoming a mother that I and other mums seem to have this superhuman power of never stopping. Like literally. I could be absolutely shattered and be seeing double, yet I'm still getting up at 5am with the little one, and managing to talk in high-pitched tones all morning imitating her favourite CBeebies characters. All the while daddy dear is still knocked out in bed! We go through the whole day pushing our own thoughts to the back of our heads and everything child / work-related gets shoved up front, fully consuming all our time and emotional energy. That's why, as I've said, it's important to take that time out for yourself to breathe, or meditate, or relax, or pray, or... exercise.

EXERCISE

When you feel like rubbish, it's easy to turn to rubbish food to make you feel better. I have tried so hard over the last few years NOT to let this happen. As you know, my relationship with food has been far from healthy, so comfort food becomes my plunging spiral. This then adds to the stress I already have because I'm trying to come to terms with all the weight I think I've put on from a few nights of bingeing on junk. That's the last thing I need – more stress!

It sounds clichéd, but I find that exercise really is a great 'de-stresser'. Now that doesn't mean having to go insane in the gym for hours on end. A ten-minute workout in the comfort of my living room is just the trick! Absolutely any form of physical exercise where I've managed to build up a minor sweat ('minor' being the key word here) takes a huge weight off my shoulders. It genuinely helps me to keep things in check, as I feel as though I've salvaged some form of control, even if that feeling only lasts a few hours.

I'd suggest doing a 10-minute exercise, three or four times a week. Or if routine exercise is boring for you, why not stick on some music and dance off those calories? It's way more fun, and you can work on nailing some new and impressive moves! For me, though, one of the best forms of exercise is going for a walk in the countryside or even hiking up a hill – you can't beat taking in the natural surroundings and fresh air! It's great for the body, mind and soul.

SOCIETY

'Nothing is heavier on the scales than beautiful character.'

Prophet Muhammad
(peace and blessings be upon him)

GETTING REAL WITH HIJAB

As I've mentioned earlier, adopting the wearing of a headscarf supposedly means you focus on character instead of looks; that people won't judge you on your physical appearance but on the 'beauty from within' and all that clichéd stuff. Yet, ironically, the women around me – the family friends and girls my age – seem to concentrate more on how they look as a 'hijabi' and are judged for their religiousness.

As I've grown older, I've realised this attitude amongst some Muslims in regards to hijab wearers and non-wearers doesn't change. Not one little bit. It's almost as though hijabis are expected to be the face of Islam. In a way, I guess we are. But that doesn't mean we're not human and can't make mistakes, or that we deserve harsher judgement from members of the community. A woman wearing a headscarf is in no way more religious than a woman without one. Believe it or not, it took me a good few years to understand that concept myself. In fact, whenever I have worn more traditionally religious clothes, I have felt a sense of pride and I also garnered looks of pride from other Muslims. It's not a bad thing to take pride in your appearance, but when it can border on arrogance, then we have a problem. It's like some people are sweeping around with their faith on parade. And we should question that, because then how modest are you being? That's the opposite of modesty, surely!

To me, adopting modesty is a way of life, one that incorporates humble attitudes. And life is also about a journey; women evolve and transition depending on the societies and context in which they live and are brought up, and the personal development that they embrace.

There is a lot of judgement when it comes to women and the way they dress. It's almost ingrained into an overarching global culture that expects women to look a certain way, largely determined by male standards. We know this is happening in western societies and has been for centuries, yet when I've been taught that head-covering should protect us from that culture of superficiality, but then find my peers judging my outer 'religious' appearance, I find it hypocritical. It's just as damaging for a young girl to experience. Girls and women everywhere, Muslim or not, end up feeling overly conscious of the way they look. They are two sides of the same coin. For Muslim women, they face the constant pressure of perfecting the 'ideal' woman's image on their heads.

Let me make one point very clear: this mentality is in no way Islamic. It's cultural. I know ladies who are white British, Pakistani, North African, European and plenty of others who have similar ways of thinking when it comes to the 'ideal image'. But that doesn't make it right.

We need to keep talking about it – about the wonderful diversity that exists among all women and how they *choose* to dress. We need to encourage more conversation, to be more tolerant, to be more understanding that there is no one way to represent a Muslim woman.

SKIN DEEP

I grew up with the strong Egyptian sunshine and the sun-kissed seaside of the English coastline, so for me, getting a tan was inevitable. Having an olive skin tone already meant we caught the sun pretty easily. Yet my cousins who were full Egyptian would think their lives were over if they caught even the slightest bit of colour on their skin. Getting darker in Egypt was not considered a good look. So there you had my sister and I not really caring or even thinking about our skin colour, and my cousins practically refusing to go out in the sun for fear of getting a shade darker.

I saw the same attitude among some of my Asian friends in the UK during high school years. Not so much the refusal of going out on a hot day – because let's face it, we barely get those days here anyway – but in other ways. They'd use foundations that were too light for their skin tone, and use a flash when taking a picture to lighten their complexion. They even went to the extent of using skin bleaching products, which of course are illegal and incredibly dangerous. Yet this was considered normal for them – their mums, aunties and relatives used them, so why wouldn't they use them too? They would never openly say they wanted to be fairer, but a lot of girls don't realise essentially that what they're striving for is 'white beauty'. It's so heavily advertised as the ideal beauty in almost every single country on this planet – Japan, India, Egypt, you name it.

Although I wish we were a nation that has managed to tackle racism by now, I do strongly believe it's ingrained so deep into the minds of some that they don't even realise the prejudice they're exuding any more. It's taken the incredibly subtle form of micro aggressions, leaving the recipient doubting their intuition and almost feeling guilty for thinking that these 'lovely white people have accidentally offended me, I'd better not say anything as they didn't mean any harm'. So you can imagine the frustration some people feel when a white person enjoys getting a tan to achieve that 'healthy glow' – which some people even call a form of appropriation – yet that same person might not respect people of an 'ethnic minority' with naturally darker skin tones.

Why is having tanned skin when you're originally white, suddenly glamorous? I guess it's only glamorous when you have white features to pair it with, not brown-person features, right? This tanned person can enjoy their 'beautified' skin tone, having never experienced the racism and bigotry that comes with having naturally dark skin. And they will never have to deal with being treated differently because of their skin colour.

I know a lot of people might be thinking at this point, but isn't it also appropriation when brown or black people bleach their skin? No, it's not. You can't embed, oppress and brainwash the idea of white beauty on to people's psyche for centuries, then turn around and condemn them for striving to be socially accepted by trying to achieve what's been drummed into them as the 'norm' while yearning for equal human rights.

And let's not gloss over the fact that many Muslims are racist towards black Muslims. In Egypt, it's grossly obvious. Egyptians use the word – *abd*, or *abeed*, meaning slave. When you call them out on it, they get so offended, deflect and turn themselves in to victims! And then you see racism when it comes to marriage. It's very rare to see Asians marry black Muslims, for example, but it should be normal. You even see racism in the Muslim fashion world. We constantly advertise women wearing headscarfs but how many of our black sisters are represented within these platforms too? I know it happens across mainstream fashion as well, but it shouldn't be happening in the modest fashion scene AT ALL. In general, black Muslims are not represented enough in the Muslim communities. We need to listen to all voices in order to reflect our communities properly.

It's taken me a while to realise that it's all of our duties and responsibility to educate ourselves on things like this. Make the changes instead of waiting for them to be made.

As a fair-skinned person, I won't ever be patronising and say, 'Just be comfortable in your skin', because I don't face the same prejudice day in day out, like many other people. But I will say this: we need education. We need to educate our kids to understand that every colour is beautiful, that there is no 'norm'. I am hopeful as the youth are so awake, and they're constantly having conversations that challenge narrow-minded attitudes. Social media has encouraged and facilitated the debate, and if our younger generation becomes more open-minded, it will have a trickle-down effect, so that the next generation will be even more aware, and then the next, and so on, meaning these old attitudes will eventually die out.

GENDER WARS

When it comes to gender stereotyping within our own communities, I think we're all guilty of it to some extent – even me. When I was pregnant, I was worried that if it were a girl, how would I bring her up when girls are generally more vulnerable than boys in lots of different situations? How would I ensure her safety at all times? There seems to be so much to protect her from. But then I wondered if that's stereotyping. We should be equally as worried when it comes to boys because at the end of the day children are children, and both sexes go through vulnerable stages in life. We, as parents and guardians, should be more aware of things, whether or not people deem you 'paranoid'. This is another thing that really grinds my gears, especially since becoming a mum – when people label my genuine worries for my child as paranoia. Any concerns I have or precautions I take with my child seem to be laughed at amongst my relatives and even some of my viewers – although most are amazingly supportive. But there are more and more challenges facing our children today, and we all have to be prepared to navigate them.

I went into a toy shop recently to pick up a few presents for Hana's cousins. Upon entering the store, I noticed one great big dividing factor that set me right off. The colour scheme, of course. One half of the shop was blue and the other bright pink. I genuinely couldn't believe that I was witnessing such utter crap. I proceeded to scour the disturbingly pink aisles, investigating further that the teddies and dolls on offer to our little girls were dressed in little crop tops and short shorts, almost knicker length! Here we are in the twenty-first century, enforcing the sexualisation of our children from as young as six months old. Some teddies are even fashioned in tees with 'princess' or 'pretty' or 'love' plastered across the front. Why do I even need to explain what's wrong with this? All I know is that I felt so much frustration, anger and more than anything utter fear for the society that seems as backdated as ever. A society that my daughter will grow up in. We still have to fight the fight that women have been fighting for years.

'I'm a feminist.
I've been a female for
a long time now.
It'd be stupid not to be
on my own side.'

Maya Angelou

BOYS TO MEN?

While growing up with my two younger brothers, my sister and I witnessed so many differences in our upbringing. There were certain things my sister and I weren't allowed to do, but my brothers were given the green light. In general, it was clear that my brothers were given a lot more freedom, and earlier on. Don't get me wrong, I'm not bitter about it at all, in fact I think compared to plenty of my friends, I had a lot of freedom. But I do find it interesting and a little unfair that my brothers were less under the thumb. As much as I understand safety issues, it's concerning that lots of family households have similar dynamics, too. I believe the problem lies in confusing and justifying some cultural traditions with religion, to the extent that they are oppressive towards girls. Yet, surprise surprise, there seems to be no education or logical reasoning behind it. In stark contrast, or double standards I should say, it's those same 'traditions' that seem to absolve the boys of any wrongdoing. I feel that this zero-discipline approach turns many of these young Muslim boys into adults who are incapable of having a healthy relationship. This in turn leads to more problems than we can seem to identify, let alone tackle.

Let's talk about dating for a moment, and the Muslim girlfriend / boyfriend scene. Too many times I've heard of a Muslim girl getting caught with her boyfriend, and her life is over. In some cases, I unfortunately mean that literally. In many other cases, the girl's reputation in the community is ruined and she is subject to misogynistic labelling, harsh judgement from female elders and a swiftly arranged marriage with a cousin from back home. She is likely to have zero freedom. And what about the consequence for the boyfriend? Absolutely nothing. This is blatant sexism, and it makes no sense. On the positive side, there are cases, more and more now in fact with the millennial generation, that the couple are given parental blessing and they live happily ever after (or a version of it!).

I think it's so important to educate our girls and our boys right from day dot. We need to teach them to respect all people in general. It's less about separating and singling out respect for girls and women – it's more about respect in general for HUMAN BEINGS.

MARRIAGE CRISIS

We have a crisis on our hands – many Muslims are finding it really hard to get married. There are so many reasons for this, I won't go into all of them but I will touch on some. For instance, let's consider the matchmaking services, which are often part of a mosque. These services are run by a much older generation (the uncles and aunties) who seem completely out of touch with what the youth are looking for in a life partner.

In reaction to that – and from the rejection of it – we have ended up with the rise of the 'Muslim dating scene', as mentioned above. Technically, Muslims aren't meant to date before marriage, but let's get real, how else are young people going to find a partner and figure out what a person is like? But the 'dating' scene has its own issues – some single Muslims get used to serial dating and don't actually make the commitment. Plus, as there are no parents or senior community members involved, it means less accountability.

Another issue is chasing the 'perfect' partner. A lot of young people have a fixed idea of what they want, which can be fine of course. But when you are so set on where your future partner will be from, what he will look like, what career he must be in and so forth, you end up missing out on what could have been the perfect person had you just seen beyond your not-very-important checklist. I know this is easier said than done, when half of your reasons for wanting those specifics might be to please your parents, but if it's not this generation that respectfully and rightfully stands up for themselves, then which generation will and how will there ever be change?

Cultural background is another barrier that many Muslims have created for themselves. If you've met someone who ticks all your boxes except for one – that they're not from the same race or culture as you, do NOT let this stop you. If you are reluctant, you really need to re-evaluate what you want in life, because essentially what you're choosing is to stay closed in a box that you know as your 'safe place'. But if you do that, you'll never know how amazing your life could be with someone with whom you can share, teach and learn new experiences. Not to mention the beautiful mix of cultures your children can enjoy! As you can tell, I'm a real advocate for interracial marriage!

I can't say I've got any tips on where to find a potential partner other than the usual environments like university, work or through friends. I do believe,

though, that it's not something you should particularly go out seeking. Of course, have an open mindset with people you might meet, because nothing happens without a little bit of effort, right? What I mean is, you don't necessarily need to go on the 'hunt'. When it's time, things happen organically for you, whatever is meant to be, will be.

TYING THE KNOT

Let's rewind a little to earlier on in my life – to me attempting to get married. After four very long, exhausting years and many arguments, my dad finally gave us his blessing. It was just before Christmas in December 2012. I think both Sid and I were more relieved than happy, as we could finally start planning our lives together. For the next year we began organising our wedding and getting a flat sorted. We got married on 1 September 2013 in a beautiful manor house in Wales.

I'm not going to lie; my wedding day was NOT the happiest day of my life. It was hell, I hated it, and so did Sid. The run up to it was so stressful with ridiculous amounts of family clashes and arguments, and the night before we'd had a HUGE argument ourselves. However, everyone else seemed to love our wedding! They said it was the best wedding they had been to, because it was a fun and gorgeous fusion of our cultures. We had traditional drumming, British food, and, of course, Egyptian dancing fused with a bit of bhangra here and there!

Believe it or not I'm actually not one for the spotlight and felt so uncomfortable with all eyes on the bride. I couldn't wait until it was over so we could take a deep breath and relax on honeymoon.

Relax we did. Of course we both suffered from the expected nerves of spending the day and night together, but overall it was a lovely time away. I even vlogged about it, which Sid wasn't too happy about. At that time he really wasn't into the idea of uploading our lives on YouTube. In fact, he's only really been open to that in the last couple of years, and trust me it took a lot of persuading! Sid has been there since Day One – he set up my Facebook page, was always taking my pictures, and was always behind the scenes before we got married. It took me ages to persuade him to be on camera after we tied the knot. When we look back at those first videos, it's like he's a different person! But he's so comfortable now, and a lot more natural. We even decided to do a joint channel, uploading vlogs on coupley stuff, and that's how we got into making advice and family-related videos.

But, here's my warning sign to all pending wives and husbands: the first year of marriage really isn't what you'll expect. It can be serious hell. You may well threaten your partner with divorce almost daily, witness the demon you never knew you had in you and you will likely not get on with your in-laws.

But do not fear, because once you get through that and you're halfway into your second year, then marriage can be great. (For the most part!)

NO SEX PLEASE, WE'RE MUSLIM

Let me first paint a scene – a sex scene to be precise. The kind that takes you unawares in the middle of *EastEnders* and you're frantically trying to change the channel with shifting eyes to and from your dad's death stare. You feel the temperature of the room rise while his angry embarrassment simmers up past his ears ready to burst at the sound of another televised snog or grunt. All the while, your mum is calmly but firmly ordering you to 'change the channel'. She repeats this instruction numerous times within the next ten chaotic seconds with that undertone of threat, as if to imply that you secretly wanted to watch this dirty sex scene in front of your parents. Meanwhile, you're wishing the carpet would swallow you up already before they think you're into pornos (but really just *EastEnders* snog scenes). You're wondering where the hell the 'effin remote went, when you could have sworn it was between your knees under your bowl of biscuits like ten flipping minutes ago??!! And that's generally a young Muslim's awkward introduction to sex.

I wish it wasn't the case but the ultimate goal for a lot of Muslim girls always seems to be marriage. I was no exception. I dreamed of the day I would find my husband and would sit preoccupied with what he might look like. I was still an innocent kid even as a teenager. When I 'fancied' a boy it was just admiration of a handsome face. It wasn't until my late high school years that I even knew what sex was, even though everyone around me, minus our circle of friends, was losing their virginity like it was their bus pass. I would also worry relentlessly about having the perfect figure for my husband, but then also have mini panic attacks about the thought of letting anyone ever see me naked. As Muslims, dating is kinda frowned upon, so for some of us, even talking to a guy we liked seemed naughty as hell. Imagine going from having never been in a relationship to suddenly being married and moving in?! You're barely given the opportunity to ask questions about sex or relationships, and now you're supposed to be intimate with your husband!

Sex is such a taboo topic amongst Muslims and to go from not having any kind of physical relationship with the guy you love to suddenly living with him, IS very daunting! That goes for Muslim men, too, who have never had any experience and have to defer to the movies to find out what sex is all about. Or if they've been really naughty, porn – which raises loads of red flags around sexual relationships. It's no wonder we have so many issues within our communities. The bottom line is we need to TALK MORE. Stop being embarrassed to talk about things that are natural and that we're expected to experience. To any parents reading this, we need to educate our kids on all the things we were ever worried about growing up, no matter how 'inappropriate'. We can't censor the youth and it's better they get the correct information from adults they trust than from some random Google search.

Also, a warning about attitudes towards marriage: if any young girl is reading this and thinks getting married is the 'be all and end all' of life, please stop. Stop and start living your life NOW. Whilst marriage should be a beautiful union between two people, let me tell you it's not going to be what you thought it would be. You won't be able to do ALL you ever dreamed of, so start living your dreams now. If you concentrate on your passions, you will grow as a person. In fact, you can pick a life partner much better that way. It is nice to grow together, but that doesn't always happen. Don't do everything to get a husband, do everything you can for you, and the husband will come, God willing.

WEDDING NIGHT MYTH

When a Muslim couple actually gets married, they have expectations of losing their virginity on the wedding night, but the reality is far from that. No one told me that it would take me a good month or so to lose my virginity after marriage. For the first couple of weeks, I actually thought there was something wrong with me. Although I'd known Sid for four years before tying the knot, going on honeymoon, moving into our first flat together and having to get to know each other on a whole new level was overwhelming enough, let alone starting a sexual relationship! I wish I had known more of what to expect and to know that it was okay to take that long to have sex. Yep, three weeks is considered a long time by the way, judging by the reaction of those closest to me! It's a weird thing to go through, because not only are you suddenly questioning your physical health in that *ahem* 'area' but you also start feeling guilty that you've 'deprived' your husband of losing his virginity as soon as he weds you! But listen up: you should *never* feel guilty for not giving up your virginity immediately. It should be known by both bride and groom (especially the groom as the pressure seems to come from them most of the time in terms of the wedding night), that it's okay to *take your time*. I honestly believe we need to have open, *safe* conversations about all this stuff. We need to have an environment where young people can ask all the questions they've ever wanted to and not worry about judgement or lecturing. All they need is a respectful and honest exchange.

THE
IN-LAWS

They say that when you marry a man, you also marry his family. Although I'd like to think I don't believe this for a second, there is some truth to it. At the end of the day, both of you need to make an effort to get to know your in-laws. You're both having to get used to a whole new family and to being comfortable around them. If one of you takes longer than the other, or is never 100 per cent comfortable, that's okay too. Be understanding and support each other on the journey.

Although our in-laws become an extension of the family, it's nothing like being with your actual family. If you are apprehensive about being yourself while not offending your in-laws, my first and most important tip would be: 'Start as you mean to go on.' Make it clear from day one the kind of person you are and where your boundaries lie. There are ways to do this without being rude or offensive.

Sometimes, though, it doesn't matter how polite you are, you'll always offend somebody, somehow. That just comes with the territory of suddenly having a larger extended family to consider, so it might feel like you really can't win on some occasions. As long as you know you haven't disrespected anyone, and vice versa, it's okay. When you nip it in the bud, it prevents interfering from the in-laws, or mind games for that matter, and means the relationship between you and your husband will be better in the long run.

Which leads me on to tip two: keep things private between you and your partner. Not just from your in-laws, but also your family. If you've had an argument over who lost the keys and it explodes into the worst argument of the century, do not go and vent to your sister about all the terrible names he called you. Your sister will remember this incident forever, whereas you'll forget about it the next day.

Plus, if there's already tension between your sister and your husband, that's not going to help and will make your spouse look terrible in their eyes. It's about keeping your arguments contained, not blowing the lid off! Every couple has arguments but it's also important to seek help from family members or professionals if your arguing turns into something more serious that can lead to danger, both emotional and physical.

To the parents out there whose children are getting married, the only thing I could advise is to throw all of your expectations of your future son / daughter-in-law out of the window. Whatever they are, it's too much pressure (other than the standard mutual respect that should exist between human beings). High expectations will only lead to disappointment, which can then lead to tension. You need to understand that when your child is marrying someone, they're also becoming part of another family as much as your new son / daughter-in-law is a part of yours. A lot of parents seem to expect the son / daughter-in-law to suddenly prioritise them over their own parents, too, which is something I've never quite got my head around, and I refuse to even be understanding of it. So, to all the in-laws on either side, my combined piece of advice to you all would be: just let each other be.

We've managed to find harmony and balance for both sides of our families over the years, and there's a good dynamic between us all now. It takes time, and it takes a hell of a lot of effort, but it does pay off in the end.

CONFIDENCE

'It's SO important to have bags of confidence and self-belief!' I hear this cliché all the time and to be honest, it sometimes prompts a mini puke in my mouth. I mean, it is true, but this advice is a bit too blasé when so many of us suffer from low self-esteem, anxiety and even panic attacks. It's much more common than we think, especially in the YouTube world.

I've been to countless events, meetings and parties thanks to being a YouTuber, but it has been daunting. Everyone thinks you'd be totally at ease with the social networking, and they expect you to do a presentation with as much confidence as you do on your channel. It was in these settings that I realised I had a problem with anxiety. At least two or three years of my blogging lifespan has been spent tackling it whenever an event arises. The bigger the opportunity, the more anxiety I'd have and the longer I would take to psych myself up for it. I couldn't count the number of times I've backed out at the last minute on what could have been amazing prospects. I would cancel the morning of my scheduled appearance, or sometimes simply not turn up (which is terribly unprofessional) and turn off any means of communication. I would literally be in hiding, then feel sorry for myself and watch daytime TV, devouring anything in the kitchen to boost my mood a little.

One episode in particular made me realise that this anxiety was essentially controlling my life and making me miserable. From the moment I was confirmed for a project, until its actual completion, I spent every moment worrying about all the things that could possibly go wrong and thinking up excuses to back out. It would consume my thoughts and niggle away 24 / 7. I pulled the classic 'Dina goes AWOL' move, but to be fair to me, I was also four months pregnant and dealing with morning sickness too. Not a good combo by any means. Anyway, they of course found a replacement for me, thanks to my anxiety and sickness, and her career was pretty much made. Yet I believe everything happens for a reason. When I think back to it now, I know there's no way in hell I would have been emotionally stable enough to deal with media interviews. Especially considering that when the project launched, I had just given birth to my baby. So on top of everything else, I was also dealing with a serious case of 'baby blues'. Having said that, it definitely gave me a reality check and prompted me to tackle my problem. From that time onwards, I made a promise to myself that I would not back out of anything I'd been confirmed for, regardless of my feelings, and that I would take every opportunity.

Since living by this general rule, my confidence has slowly started to improve. I'm also taking less and less time to psych myself up with each new project. Once each commitment is done, I'm always left feeling like I really needn't have worried and got myself so worked up about it, because, and this is important – it's never as bad as you think. Remember, I'm by no means an expert when it comes to dealing with anxiety and mental health. I'm fully aware that there are people who have to deal with it on a much more serious level than me. I'm purely sharing my personal experience with you in the hope that some of you can relate to it, and know that you're certainly not alone. Some of you may not even realise you're dealing with anxiety, I didn't myself until very recently! I thought it was just a bad case of nerves for a long, long time.

My mum always tells me to push myself
and try new things that are out of my comfort zone.
She believes this will help boost my confidence and
renew my faith that I CAN do it, whatever 'it' is.
Whilst I completely champion this theory, I also
think it's essential to stay true to yourself, even
if you've conquered doubt and are ready to tackle
whatever comes your way. What I've found recently
with the blogging sphere and myself in general, is
that sometimes it can be obvious when someone is
doing something that doesn't sit naturally with them,
and in turn it can be very uncomfortable as an outsider
to watch. It's important to remember who you are,
what you believe in – religiously or ethically – and
know what your limits are.

Once you've established yourself and your
brand, you'll start understanding that not every
opportunity is a good one. This is something that
took me a while to grasp. I went through a phase
of taking everything offered to me and didn't really
consider the future, namely whether or not it fitted
into my long-term plan and brand image. Not only
would I suggest keeping in mind your brand identity
and future plans, but also I strongly believe that
going with your gut is just as, if not more, important.
Whatever you take on has to feel right, if you feel
it compromises your morals and beliefs, even just
slightly, you'll know it's not the right gig for you.
Even if the prospects seem amazing at the time,
they'll probably be very short-lived, or you won't
be totally happy. You need the confidence and
conviction to do what is right for you.

'Let the beauty of what you love be what you do.'

Rumi

But I know only too well how much of a struggle it can be to take the path of a blogger. Blogging is not the easiest job on the planet. And contrary to popular belief, you don't live like a celebrity, because we're not! I'm not famous, I'm a regular person who has passion and who struggles through life, and who pays bills, just like you. Yeah, the pressure might get to me sometimes, it can be intimidating if I go to an area like East London where lots of my Muslim audience live and may recognise me from YouTube or Instagram. But the reality is so different to what that tiny camera on my mobile phone can project. Still, I'm so grateful for the experience I've had, and the amazing support I've received from so many of you. I feel like I've come a pretty long way, and there's still so much ahead.

Dina's Final Thoughts

So, what's next for the modest fashion world, and for me, I often ask myself? I mean, I've always wanted to design clothes for women like me, but do women like me even need us small-time designers any more? Especially when we have the high street and major fashion houses doing it for us. Sometimes I get frustrated, thinking 'they're taking our jobs and claiming they invented MODEST FASHION!' Oh, the irony! Hah!

But then I pat myself on the back and say, YES, they do need people like us! Because if it wasn't for a bunch of us who took to social media to reclaim our own narratives then this might not have happened. So it should really be looked at as a success story. But what's the next chapter? Maybe I need to continue striving to figure out more positive changes that we can help make happen. Maybe it's more than just fashion. Maybe I want to address and tackle even more in my life. Maybe I just want to be a mum. Whatever it is, and this is a message to both myself and to you: go where your heart leads you and don't be afraid of your own growth, even if it's not what people want to see or what people may always want. Don't ever think your job is done, and don't ever think your job isn't important, no matter how little or trivial it might seem to others. There's always more you can offer, only you can make the right decision for *you*. Together, we've caused a revolution, and now it's time to move forward. Never doubt your worth. Hold on to your empowering stories. Name it, claim it, own it.

Okay, that was kind of deep, but I mean it girls. Just do YOU.

abayas 97, 123
acne 147
anxiety 216, 217
autumn/winter
day to night looks 115
go-to looks 114
key looks 112–13

bags 99–101, 111
base makeup 150, 160
beauty 140–65
beauty box basics 148–9
brows 155, 162
contouring 151, 161
daytime glam 160–4
eyeliners 152–3, 163
eyeshadow 154, 162–3
haircare 158–9
lashes 156–7, 163
lipstick 164
night transition
makeup 165
nightcare 146
perfecting your base 150
skincare routines 142–5
tired eyes 146
beauty blender 148
belts 115
blazers 97, 110, 137
blogging 219
hijabs and 68, 70
top tips 62–4
blotting paper 148
blusher 161
body image
eating disorders and 37
effect of hijabs on 20, 22
body shape 30–1
bottling it up 193
boys, bringing up 204–5
brands, modest fashion
and 68, 70
breastfeeding 176–7
brows 155, 162
brushes, makeup 148–9
bulimia 34–7
bullying 32–3
online bullying 41
burkinis 138, 139

careers, choosing 50–1
casual looks
autumn/winter 114
spring/summer 110
cheeks
contouring
cheekbones 151, 161
contouring
chubby cheeks 91
chiffon scarves 79
chinos 109
classic look
headscarves 85
cleansing 144
clutch bags 100
coats 95, 108
coconut oil 145, 146, 159
collars 113
concealer 150, 160, 162
confidence 42, 216–19
contour brushes 148
contouring 151, 161
cotton fabric
cotton undertops 123
cotton/viscose-blend
scarves 80

dating 205, 206, 210–11
day to night looks
autumn/winter 115
spring/summer 111
daywear
autumn/winter 115
daytime glam 160–4
spring/summer 106, 111
denim 92
DINATOKIO 58–61
dresses, layering
with shirts 120–1

eating disorders 34–7
Eid 13, 15, 125
elegant look headscarfs 85
everyday looks
brows 155, 162
everyday drape
headscarves 74
everyday 'meet me
halfway' look
headscarves 75
everyday wrap
headscarves 75

exercise 181, 194
exercise bulimia 34
eyes
brows 155, 162
daytime glam 162–3
eyeliners 152–3, 163
eyeshadow 154, 162–3
lashes 156–7, 163
tired eyes 146

fabrics
dress 127, 128
hijabs 79
face masks, DIY recipe 147
face shapes
changing with a
headscarf 90–1
styling for different 86–9
faith-based fashion 68
false eyelashes 156–7, 163
family and parenting 166–83
fashion 66–139
bags 99–101
Eid 125
fashion icons 116–17
fashion trends 118
holiday wear 132–9
key looks 106–15
maternity wear 178–9
modest fashion 68–71
proms 119–23
shopping tips 102–5
special occasions 119–39
styling headscarves
72–81, 84–91
top 10 wardrobe
essentials 92–7
turban trends 83
weddings 126–31
foreheads
narrowing big 90
softening square 90
foundation 150, 160
friends 33

gender stereotyping 202–3
girls, bringing up 204–5

hair
hair pulling 38–9
haircare 158–9
hats 109, 112
heart-shaped faces 86
hijabs and headscarves
19–30, 182–3, 196–7
acne 147
blogging and 68, 70
brands and 29
changing your face
shape with 90–1
colour 74
creating the
perfect base 76
definition 26–8
fabrics 74, 79–81
haircare and 158–9
holiday wear 138
size 74
special occasion
styles 84–5
sports hijabs 29
styling 72–81, 84–91
styling for different
face shapes 86–9
three everyday
styles 74–5
holiday wear 132–9
burkinis 138, 139
headscarves 138
jewellery 135
packing and toiletries 133
shoes 134
statements and
staples 137
hydration 144

In-laws 213–15
interracial marriage 207
Islamophobia 21

jackets 97, 110, 137
jaws, softening strong 90
jeans 92, 97, 137
jersey scarves 81
jewellery 111, 135

Kaan, Sid
marriage to Dina
52–7, 208–9
parenting 168, 169, 170, 175,
180, 183–5

knitwear 112, 113, 114
lashes 156–7
life/work balance 188–9
lipstick 164
long faces, headscarf
    styles for 87, 91
losing it 188–9

makeup
    brows 155, 162
    contouring 151, 161
    eyeliners 152–3, 163
    eyeshadow 154, 162–3
    lashes 156–7, 163
    lipstick 164
    night transition
        makeup 165
    packing for holidays 133
    perfecting your base 150
    removing 146
    tools 148–9
marriage 206–9, 211
    in-laws 213–15
    wedding night myths 212
massages 145, 146
maternity wear 178–9
mental health 177, 217
mindfulness 191
modal blend scarves 70
models 70
moisturising 145
motivation 49

necklaces 111
night transition makeup 165
nightcare of skin 146

online pressure 40–1
online shopping 105
oval faces 89

parenting 166–83
    breastfeeding 176–7
    going outside 181
    maternity wear 178–9
    putting yourself
        first 180, 190
    raising your child 182–3
    staying active 181
    support networks 172–3
    switching off the TV 181
    team effort 180
    working mums 175

peer pressure 40
post-natal depression
    168, 177
powder 150, 151, 160
prayer 191
procrastination 49
proms 119–23

racism 199–200
Ramadan
    eating disorders and 37
    fashion and 123, 125
regal look headscarves 84
relationships 54
round faces 89

sanity, keeping your 190
scarves 74, 95
    fabrics 79–81
    underscarves 159
sex 210–11, 212
shirts
    crisp white 95, 110, 114, 137
    layering for strapless
        dresses 120–1
    loose white shirts 137
    three white-shirt looks 121
shoes
    day to night looks 111
    holiday wear 134
    spring/summer
        essentials 108
    trainers 92
shopping tips 102–5
silk scarves 79
skin colour 199–201
skincare
    chin and jaw acne 147
    nightcare 146
    routines 142–5
skirts 113, 114, 137
smart looks
    autumn/winter 114
    spring/summer 110
social media 22, 40–1
    DINATOKIO 58–61
    setting boundaries 60
society 196–7
special occasions
    119–39, 155
spiritual wellbeing 191
sport hijabs 29

spring/summer
    day to night 111
    essentials 108–9
    go-to looks 110
    key looks 106
square-shaped faces 87
stereotyping, gender 202–3
stress 188, 193, 194
support networks 172–3
sweaters, oversized plain
    boyfriend 112, 114

toiletries 133
tools, make-up 148–9
tops
    breastfeeding 179
    floral 108
    oversized 94
    'saviour' black 94
    white shirts 95, 110, 114, 137
Torkia, Dina
    college years 42–3
    DINATOKIO 58–61
    early life 10–17
    eating disorder 34–7
    hair pulling 38–9
    Hana 168–73, 176–7
    hijabs 19–25
    marriage to Sid
        52–7, 208–9
    move to Britain 10–12
    move to Wales 16–17
    school 12–13, 16–17,
        30–1, 46
    siblings 12–13
    starts blogging 58, 62–3
    teenage years 19–25, 32–3
    university 46–7
    YouTube 58–60
traditional dress 123
trichotillomania 38
trousers
    chinos 109
    jeans 92, 97, 137
    maternity 178
turbans
    spring/summer 109, 110
    turban trends 83
turmeric, DIY face mask 147
TV, switching off 181
tweezers 149

underscarves 159
undertops, cotton 123

veils 129
virginity, losing 210, 212
viscose/cotton-blend
    scarves 80

wardrobe essentials,
    top 10 92–7
weddings 126–31
    brides 126–9
    guests 130
    wedding night myths 212
weekend looks
    autumn/winter 114
    spring/summer 110
wings 152, 163
winter/autumn
    day to night looks 115
    go-to looks 114
    key looks 112–13
work
    autumn/winter
        work looks 114
    spring/summer
        work looks 110
    work/life balance 188–9
    working mums 175

yoghurt, DIY face mask 147
YouTube 58–9

I never thought I'd be able to say I'm a 'published author' but thanks to the amount of positive people and incredibly supportive audience that I have in my life, I've ended up bloody well becoming one! Honestly, I can't help but pat myself on the back for finally getting there after two years of working on this book and almost giving up every other month! I've got a lot of people to thank for helping me get there in the end and I'd like to start with the girls over at Penguin who approached me in the first place with every faith that we could come up with something half decent together, despite my constant self-deprecating attitude at almost every meeting. Sorry girls but also thanks for putting up with me and encouraging me to push myself (Louise McKeever in particular, I owe you a box of chocolates or something!)

Then of course there's Flora, Louise and Jess my agents, they too didn't stop reassuring me every time I'd doubt myself. Without them being on my case about delivery deadlines I probably would have never got there, hah!

Rose, for designing this book and Claire, the photographer, for making me look great in photos! And then there's also Alessia who I've been shooting with for years, she's snapped some of my most iconic looks!

Remona Aly, my editor, who helped make sense of my ramblings during countless hour-long phone conversations, making sure that we had covered every detail – sorry if I frazzled your brain!

There's you guys, my internet family. I would never have ended up writing this book if it hadn't been for your continued support over the last ten years of my blogging life. It's crazy to think you've been on this journey with me for that long – with every new story in my life so many of you have been going through the same motions as me, it's like we're a huge network of pen pals, perhaps!

I've got my little girl Hana who made me a mama and if it wasn't for her I would have never matured into the woman that would be able to even think about writing a book. I'm so grateful for you Hana, and I hope that one day you can take something from this book. Know that it's all for you my cheeky little monkey.

Here's to Sid my husband of five years but partner of ten. Ever supporting and selfless in our marriage, you know how much I appreciate you... babes! Your support has been tremendous and I can't wait to continue growing with you and as a family of four very soon!

My twin Toosy, she's basically my best friend and the only other person on the planet that will understand every single moan I have in life, she doesn't know this guys but I look up to her a lot (especially her fashion sense!)

Finally, I'd like to thank the biggest inspiration in my life, my mum. It's cliché but since becoming a mum I can't help but thank her for everything. For dedicating her whole life to us. My mum really shaped me as a person and sometimes I sit back and think how the hell she manages to be so epic.

Thank you
xxx